NINETY
DAYS
TO
FINANCIAL
FITNESS

Money A to Z:
A Consumer's Guide to the Language of Personal Finance
Mattie's Money Tree (a juvenile by Don German)
The Only Money Book for the Middle Class
The Bank Employee's Security Handbook
The Money Book (a juvenile by Joan German)
How to Find a Job When Jobs Are Hard to Find
The Bank Teller's Handbook
Make Your Own Convenience Foods
Tested Techniques in Bank Marketing, Volume 1
Tested Techniques in Bank Marketing, Volume 2
Money & Banks (a juvenile by Don German)
Bank Employee's Marketing Handbook

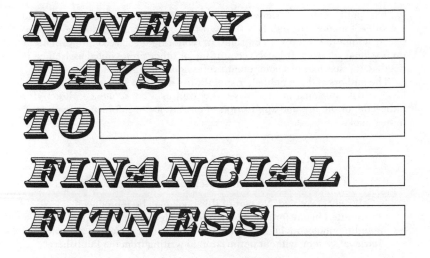

NINETY DAYS TO FINANCIAL FITNESS

Don and Joan German

COLLIER BOOKS *Macmillan Publishing Company*   New York

Copyright © 1986 by Don German and Joan German

All rights reserved. No part of this book may be reproduced or transmitted in any form or by any means, electronic or mechanical, including photocopying, recording or by any information storage and retrieval system, without permission in writing from the Publisher.

Macmillan Publishing Company
866 Third Avenue, New York, N.Y. 10022
Collier Macmillan Canada, Inc.

Library of Congress Cataloging-in-Publication Data
German, Donald R.
Ninety days to financial fitness.
Includes index.
1. Finance, Personal—United States. I. German,
Joan W.   II. Title.   III. Title: Ninety days to financial
fitness.
HG179.G463   1986   332.024   85-16814
ISBN 0-02-079620-X (pbk.)

Macmillan books are available at special discounts for bulk purchases, for sales promotions, premiums, fund-raising, or educational use. For details contact:

Special Sales Director
Macmillan Publishing Company
866 Third Avenue
New York, N.Y. 10022

Ninety Days to Financial Fitness is also available in a hardcover edition from Macmillan Publishing Company.

10 9

Designed by Jack Meserole

Printed in the United States of America

With love to Edward and Jane German—
"Buzz and Jane"

Contents

Acknowledgments

We wish to express our sincere thanks . . .

To Elizabeth Frost Knappman, president of New England Publishing Associates, Inc., for being such a good friend and, as our literary agent, for contributing so much to this book in terms of ideas, time, and support; to Alexia Dorszynski of Macmillan Publishing Company, our editor, for believing in this project and offering guidance as only a top-notch editor can, and to Jill Herbers her assistant; to Amy Weiss Bizar, vice president of the Bank of New England, for her years of warmth and generosity in sharing her vast store of banking/legal knowledge; and to all the special friends who were ready with a warm hug and a chilled glass of wine whenever they were needed during the writing of this book, especially Adelle Michaud, Arthur Phinney, and Sibylle and Bill Baughan.

PART I

QUICK FIXES FOR
FINANCIAL ILLS

Who This Book Is For
and How to Use It

Financial fitness in ninety days? Can it really be done? Most of all, can I do it?

If these are your questions, the answers are YES, YES, and YES.

Now here are two "buts":

You have to work at it a little, and . . .

Your financial problems must be solvable.

In other words, if you're on your way to jail for embezzlement, this book won't help you.

If you're divorced, earn $10,000 a year, and are the father of 13 kids and have just been ordered to pay child support for all of them, you should probably use the price of this book to buy a stiff drink. Better yet, maybe you should buy two.

Or if filing for bankruptcy every six years is your idea of asset management, save your money.

But if you're a typical person with typical money problems, this book can give you the first aid that you need, and it can help to put you on the road to financial strength.

HOW TO USE THIS BOOK

Ninety Days to Financial Fitness is divided into two parts. The first part is designed to help you get your money matters into shape as quickly as possible. The second part provides ways to maintain your financial health once any acute problems have been solved.

Start with Part I. You may want to follow several of the guidelines at the same time, using your financial strength from one chapter to go on to another. For example, you'll need to keep in mind that you should hold your credit spending down as you move on to concentrate on cutting expenses.

Each chapter in Part I is labelled with the amount of time it should take to carry out the guidelines described. Many of the changes you'll be making will take place simultaneously. The plan will show you how to do it easily and without headaches. A handy calendar is provided at the very beginning of the book so you can check off items as you progress step-by-step through the ninety days of your financial self-improvement program. The "nonbudget" in Chapter 10 will help you see where your money is going to *keep* you in shape, but you may also flip to it as you go along if it helps you keep up with how your money is spent *while* you're following the plan.

An added note—this book is designed to help you, not to rule your financial life, so feel free to skip around or even to skip over any of the material, depending on your needs.

Finally, each chapter ends with a few observations based on the authors' many years of experience as advisers on practical money matters. Titled "Germans' Laws," they are designed to give you a chuckle as well as to remind you of some of the guidelines in each chapter. Money is only a tool to use for your benefit—so enjoy it!

Specifically, *this book is for you if:*

· You sometimes seem to have more month than you do money
· You don't know how much you really owe
· You work for a living and manage your own money

· You are nervous about applying for a loan
· You have hangups about money matters
· You are a woman suffering from wage discrimination
· You spend too much on insurance
· You charge too much on credit cards
· You don't have enough in savings or investments
· You can't seem to get a handle on cash management
· You are married and want a financial plan for the future
· You might face a divorce or separation and don't want to part with your money
· You are or might be involved in an unmarried, live-in relationship
· You are or plan to be a parent

Do you fit into any of these categories? If so, read on.

Your Personal Ninety-Day Fitness Calendar

Day	What to Do	Check Off Here
1—Monday	Get started. Complete your Financial Fitness Profile (see Chapter 1).	☐
2—Tuesday	Go on a money diet. Immediately, cut as many expenses as you can (see Chapters 2 and 5).	☐
3—Wednesday	Don't hang onto money drainers. Cut your financial losses (see Chapter 2).	☐
4—Thursday	Face your debts. Consider refinancing so you can get caught up (see Chapter 2).	☐
5—Friday	Can you sell a service or something you own? Plan to tap your assets if you can (see Chapter 2).	☐
6 and 7—Saturday and Sunday	Even God took a rest after a week of work. Take the weekend off, but don't charge your fun.	☐
8—Monday	Take the Debt Condition Test (see Chapter 3) and don't get upset—you're not alone.	☐

9—Tuesday	Rate your Credit Spending Fitness (see Chapter 3).	☐
10—Wednesday	Think about it—why are you out of shape? Don't kid yourself; be very honest (see Chapter 3).	☐
11—Thursday	Fill in the Creditor Work Sheet (see Chapter 3).	☐
12—Friday	Start contacting your creditors. Don't panic; they can be very helpful (see Chapter 3).	☐
13 and 14— Saturday and Sunday	Another weekend— relax. You're financially stronger already! Still don't charge your fun.	☐
15—Monday	Keep contacting creditors.	☐
16—Tuesday	Make further creditor contacts. Still don't panic.	☐
17—Wednesday	Look at your credit cards. Resolve to master MasterCard; don't be a victim of Visa. And don't be fooled. Credit cards are designed to make it easy to keep you spending—and in debt.	☐

Day	What to Do	Check Off Here
18—Thursday	Compute how much you spend a year in credit-card interest costs. Then don't get mad, get even—pay your credit-card bills in full when they're due (see Chapter 4).	☐
19—Friday	If you charge too much, hide your credit cards or give them to someone else to hold for you. If you're really an addict, send them back. You can get them again when you're ready to handle them.	☐
20 and 21—Saturday and Sunday	Have a quiet weekend. Don't spend money, yet.	☐
22—Monday	Start paying off your outstanding credit card balances. And, if you're "loaned up," don't use your cards.	☐
23—Tuesday	Figure out what your major expenses are and list them (see Chapter 5).	☐

24—Wednesday   Calculate how much you should be spending on housing. Keep up with your needs, not with an image. ☐

25—Thursday   If you're spending too much for housing, consider moving to a less expensive place. But don't expect this to be easy—it does hurt. ☐

26—Friday   Try to reduce property insurance costs. Almost everyone can save here (see Chapter 5)! ☐

27 and 28— Saturday and Sunday   Time off again. Still don't use those credit cards, though. ☐

29—Monday   Try to reduce your property taxes. No luck here if you rent; but if you own, you may be able to do it. ☐

30—Tuesday   Consider rewriting your mortgage, especially if you have a fixed mortgage at a high rate (see Chapter 5). ☐

31—Wednesday   Look at your insurance costs. You probably spend too much (see Chapter 5). ☐

Day	What to Do	Check Off Here
32—Thursday	Consider your life insurance plan. Can you revise it and save money (see Chapter 5)?	☐
33—Friday	See if you can save on health insurance. Consider joining an HMO (see Chapter 5).	☐
34 and 35— Saturday and Sunday	Weekend break.	☐
36—Monday	Try to save on auto insurance. Don't buy unnecessary collision coverage (see Chapter 5).	☐
37—Tuesday	Tally your auto expenses.	☐
38—Wednesday	Decide whether you can afford your car. Don't be afraid to trade down.	☐
39—Thursday	See if you can save on auto repairs by doing some of them yourself.	☐
40—Friday	Look at your overall spending habits. You may be wasting money. Where can you cut down?	☐

41 and **42**—   Take the weekend off . . .
Saturday   inexpensively.
and Sunday   □

43—Monday   Start carrying only
enough cash to get
through the day. Don't
use plastic!   □

44—Tuesday   If you smoke, quit. You
can do it!   □

45—Wednesday   Make the decision to
shop for sales from
now on. Don't buy on
impulse!   □

46—Thursday   Reduce your restaurant
spending. Give your-
self a break today—eat
at home.   □

47—Friday   Stop buying lottery tickets. Don't be a sucker
for the state!   □

48 and **49**—   You've lost a lot of finan-
Saturday   cial flab. Take a week-
and Sunday   end break and get
ready to start building
your money muscle.   □

50—Monday   Take a look in your inner
mirror. How is your fi-
nancial self-image (see
Chapter 6)?   □

Day	What to Do	Check Off Here
51—Tuesday	This is soul-searching day. If you are a woman, ask yourself if you feel financially equal to the men you know. If you are a man, ask yourself if you put women down financially. How can you improve?	☐
52—Wednesday	Try to see yourself as others see you. Are you financially stereotyped? If so, try to change your image.	☐
53—Thursday	Consider whether you have any of the negative money attitudes that appear in Chapter 6. Can you change them?	☐
54—Friday	Now that you know your weaknesses, get ready to exercise. Start by paying any bills when due—not early, when due.	☐
55 and 56—Saturday and Sunday	Take these two days off. You've had a big week.	☐

57—Monday   Visit your bank. If you
don't know the
manager, introduce
yourself and get ac-
quainted. If you don't
have a bank, find one.   ☐

58—Tuesday   Switch all of your accounts to the bank
you've chosen. This is
a chance to score some
financial points.   ☐

59—Wednesday   If it's feasible to do so,
switch all your insur-
ance to one broker.   ☐

60—Thursday   Begin to make all of your
security transactions
through one broker.   ☐

61—Friday   Work on being important
to your banker, insur-
ance agent, and broker
—refer at least one
friend to each. Feel
and act financially
strong.   ☐

62 and **63**—   Weekend break.
Saturday
and Sunday   ☐

64—Monday   This is a grim but re-
warding task—begin to
figure out how you can
cut your taxes (see
Chapter 7).   ☐

65—Tuesday   Figure your marginal tax
bracket (see Chapter 7).   ☐

Day	What to Do	Check Off Here
66—Wednesday	List all of your possible tax deductions, using the work sheet in Chapter 7. Be careful —every dollar you save is yours to keep!	☐
67—Thursday	See if you can use any legal tricks to lower your taxes. Don't assume that all such tricks are unethical (see Chapter 7).	☐
68—Friday	See how many tax shelters or deferrals you can use, referring to the list in Chapter 7. These aren't just for the wealthy.	☐
69 and 70— Saturday and Sunday	You should have saved at least $500 on taxes. Take the weekend off and buy yourself a bottle of bubbly to celebrate!	☐
71—Monday	Now it's time to put on some financial weight. Start your savings plan today, using the chart in Chapter 8. But don't try to save too much too soon; the trick to successful saving is regularity.	☐

72—Tuesday   Open a savings account,
                if you don't already
                have one. If you do
                have one, make a
                deposit.   ☐

73—Wednesday   Revise your W-4 (tax ex-
                emption form) at your
                personnel office so that
                you don't get a tax re-
                fund. Plan to bank the
                extra pay you get.   ☐

74—Thursday   If you have trouble sav-
                ing, go back to the per-
                sonnel office and sign
                up for a bond-a-month
                plan.   ☐

75—Friday   If you have a loan paid
                off, make arrangements
                to save the amount
                you're used to paying
                out each month. Avoid
                treating the extra as a
                bonus to waste.   ☐

76 and 77—   Don't you feel great?
Saturday   Take two days off.
and Sunday   ☐

78—Monday   Become an instant thou-
                sandaire by following
                the Instant Savings
                Plan in Chapter 8. It
                works!   ☐

Day	What to Do	Check Off Here
79—Tuesday	Increase your savings potential by investing what you've saved from cutting insurance costs.	☐
80—Wednesday	You're in good shape now. Your debts are under control; you have a positive money attitude; you have a working savings plan. Now learn how to borrow quickly and cheaply by following the tips in Chapter 9. But don't borrow unless you must.	☐
81—Thursday	Improve your financial health by setting up a Money Management Fitness Plan (see Chapter 10).	☐
82—Friday	Determine your Money Anxiety Level. Remember to avoid any money plan that will worry you.	☐
83 and 84— Saturday and Sunday	This week should have made you feel downright righteous. Celebrate!	☐

85—Monday	Decide what you want your money to do for you, using the work sheet in Chapter 10. This is your blueprint for the future.	☐
86—Tuesday	Make up a nonbudget, using the chart in Chapter 10.	☐
87—Wednesday	Make a plan to build your net worth. How can you buy a home? Or, if you have a home, how can you save in high-yield certificates of deposit?	☐
88—Thursday	Open an Individual Retirement Account at your bank or brokerage office. It's a great way to save and to cut taxes. Don't fail to do this—it's the most important tip in this book!	☐
89—Friday	Start an estate plan by calling your lawyer to draw up your will. If you already have a will, make sure it's up-to-date.	☐
90—Saturday	Feel good about your financial fitness and . . . live happily ever after!	☐

Rate Your Financial Fitness
(one day)

How do you rate financially? To make a physical comparison, are you the classic 98-pound weakling who must tolerate having sand kicked in your face? Or are you the strong man who can ring the bell at the carnival every time? Are you the woman who can run a marathon in under three hours? Or do you get pooped just turning TV channels?

These people have their financial counterparts. The weakling is at the mercy of moneylenders, bill collectors, and even salespeople who offer things that everyone must have and who keep the financially unfit at their mercy. The financial bell ringer, on the other hand, can walk into any bank and make a favorable deal and can negotiate with salespeople at an advantage. The marathon runner can laugh at bill collectors as she paces through life, knowing that she's fast and that she has great financial stamina. And the person who tires easily may appear financially secure on the surface, but will run out of steam at the least exertion of his or her resources.

YOUR PERSONAL FINANCIAL PROFILE

How's your financial fitness? Following is a simple test that can help you find out. Taking it will require a pencil (with an eraser, since you may have to revise a figure now and then), a look at your last income tax return, and a glance at some of your financial documents or a reasonably good memory. Some of the figures with which you will be working are based on certain premises that will be explained after you have determined your rating.

Financial Fitness Profile

First, determine the value of each of the items listed below and write each amount in the space provided at the right. Use the current fair market value, not the price you paid or the amount you invested. Then add up all the amounts to get your total.

Cash, including your checking account	$	.
Savings, including CDs		.
Balances in IRA, Keogh, or other funded retirement plans		.
Savings bonds		.
Market value of owned real estate		.
Cash value of life insurance		.
Money market mutual funds		.
Securities, including mutual funds		.
Personal property		.
Money owed to you	+	.
Total Owned	$	.

Next, find the total amount that you owe:

Mortgage loan(s) outstanding	$	.
Auto loan(s)		.
Personal loan(s)		.
Credit-card balance(s)		.
Other loan(s) due		.
Outstanding bills		.
Money owed to others	+	.
Total Owed	$	.

Now, subtract Total Owed from Total Owned:

Total Owned	$	.
− Total Owed		.
This is your Personal Net Worth	$	.

Write your Personal Net Worth in Box A, which appears after the next calculation.

Next, get your last federal income tax return and look for the adjusted gross income figure. This is the last figure on the first page of Forms 1040 and 1040A; it appears in the middle of the page on Form 1040EZ. This figure will be the basis for computing your financial fitness. Now write in the amounts for the following information in the spaces provided:

Amount of your last year's adjusted gross income	(a) $	.
Amount you deposited during that tax year to an IRA, Keogh Plan, or other funded retirement plan	+(b) $	.
Now, add (a) and (b)	$	.
Multiply the total by .35	×	.35
	$	.
Multiply the result by 6	×	6
This is your Asset Factor	$	.

Write your Asset Factor in Box B below.

BOX A Your Personal Net Worth $.	BOX B Your Asset Factor $.

These are the key factors in your Financial Fitness Rating.

Now here's the way to use these figures to rate yourself.

First, make an age adjustment for your Personal Net Worth. This is necessary because, as you get older, your net worth should grow. For example, it would be unfair to make net worth comparisons between people aged 25 and those aged 50. After all, the older you are, the more the earnings on your savings and investments should have compounded, and, while the monthly payments on your mortgage may be the same, the equity in it and your other assets will have grown at an increasing rate. Here's how to make that adjustment:

Your Personal Net Worth from Box A $_____.

If your age is 25 to 29, multiply that figure by 1.75; for age 30 to 34, multiply by 1.5; for age 35 to 39, by 1.25; for 55 to 59, by .75; and for age 60 and up, multiply by .50. If your age is between 40 and 54, leave the figure as it is. ×_____.

Age-Adjusted Net Worth $_____.

Enter your Age-Adjusted Net Worth and your Asset Factor in the boxes below:

BOX B Your Asset Factor (from above) $.	BOX C Your Age-Adjusted Net Worth $.

Now to find your Financial Fitness Rating. Using the following table, find your Asset Factor range in the first column. Then, reading across, find your approximate Age-Adjusted Net Worth. Your rating is at the top of that column.

Financial Fitness Ratings

ASSET FACTOR	AGE-ADJUSTED NET WORTH				
	Excellent	Very Good	Good	Fair	Poor
$ 25,000	$ 50,000	$ 37,500	$ 25,000	$ 18,750	$ 12,500
30,000	60,000	45,000	30,000	22,500	15,000
35,000	70,000	52,500	35,000	26,250	17,500
40,000	80,000	60,000	40,000	30,000	20,000
45,000	90,000	67,500	45,000	33,750	22,500
50,000	100,000	75,000	50,000	37,500	25,000
60,000	120,000	90,000	60,000	45,000	30,000
70,000	140,000	105,000	70,000	52,500	35,000
80,000	160,000	120,000	80,000	60,000	40,000
90,000	180,000	135,000	90,000	67,500	45,000
100,000	200,000	150,000	100,000	75,000	50,000
110,000	220,000	165,000	110,000	82,500	55,000
120,000	240,000	180,000	120,000	90,000	60,000
130,000	260,000	195,000	130,000	97,500	65,000
140,000	280,000	210,000	140,000	105,000	70,000
150,000	300,000	225,000	150,000	112,500	75,000
175,000	350,000	262,500	175,000	131,250	87,500
200,000	400,000	300,000	200,000	150,000	100,000

Here's how the table works:

As you must have noticed, you earn a "Good" rating if your Asset Factor equals your Age-Adjusted Net Worth. This is because the table is based on the following premises:

1. *The maximum debt ratio that Americans can safely carry, counting home mortgage payments, is 35 percent of gross income.*

2. *According to the Federal Reserve, the average American has a net worth equal to six times his or her debt load.* Thus, to arrive at your Asset Factor, you multiplied the total of your adjusted gross income plus cur-

rent retirement savings by .35 (which gave you your allowable debt factor), and then multiplied this result by six to arrive at your Asset Factor (or median probable net worth).

3. *The age adjustment was made to allow for the fact that people should save some money each year as well as acquire assets that add to net worth.* Thus, a person age 25 with an Asset Factor of $25,000 and an Age-Adjusted Net Worth of $25,000 (which would be a real net worth of $14,285) would rate a "Good," whereas a person aged 55 with an Asset Factor of $25,000 would have to have a real net worth of $33,333 to earn the same rating.

4. The range from "Excellent" to "Poor" is based on actual surveys and many interviews with bankers and other financial professionals, all of which attest to the fact that *in money matters,* at least, *all people are certainly not equal.* People range from money fitness freaks to those who are financially unfit, just as people's physical condition ranges from those who keep in marathon training, to those who jog several miles a day, to the average people who watch their weight and walk to work, to those who are a bit overweight and walk occasionally, down to the physical pits—the people who smoke, drink, and walk only to the refrigerator for another beer.

UNIVERSAL PROBLEMS

Everyone faces certain financial problems, regardless of their financial fitness status. One is continuing inflation. If, for example, your Age-Adjusted Net Worth is high because you inherited the money and you now have it squirreled away in a cookie jar, you should get it working in investments in which earnings exceed the inflation rate. Otherwise, if you assume a quite realistic inflation rate of just 4 percent per year, each $1,000 in net worth you have now will be worth only $664.83 in purchasing power in just 10 years!

The second universal problem involves the fact that government programs have been and will continue to be cut. Social Security, the golden crutch on which so many have relied, is fast becoming a shaky, wooden cane. Thousands of people have been purged from the disability rolls; and retirement ages are going to be moved up while taxes are increased and benefits are decreased. Medicare and Medicaid will be cut even more. One serious proposal, for example, would establish hospital wards with reduced nursing and medical staffs for people without private resources. In a nation that is likely to be divided in services between the haves and have-nots, you should take steps to insure that you number among the haves by building and maintaining a solid net worth.

PERSONAL FINANCIAL PROBLEMS

At this point, you either feel wonderful, satisfied, or depressed about your financial fitness status. If your score was "Excellent," keep up the good work—you've been doing something right. If it was "Very Good," pat yourself on the back, then get busy trying to raise your level to "Excellent." If it was "Good," congratulations —you're average; you get a "C" in the course, but you can and should do better. For a "Fair," skip the pats altogether; you pass, but barely. And for a "Poor," get busy!

Before you can raise yourself from any level, however, you must first understand the causes for your problems. And there are only two causes for money problems —too little income or too much expense.

Too Little Income

A study that appeared in the May 1981 issue of *Psychology Today* showed some amazing results. At every income level, people thought they would be able to do just fine financially if they could move up just one step. Thus, the people who earned $10,000 a year aspired to earn $20,000; those who earned from $20,000 to $30,000 a year sought $30,000 to $50,000. Their feelings were consistent; the grass was always much greener just one notch up.

But these people were wrong. Certainly, it would be nice to earn more, but chances are, in most cases, they simply spent too much, a fact that would always keep them just one level short of success.

Of course, there are people who do earn too little. Women, for example, on the average earn about 60 cents for every dollar earned by men in comparable jobs. This has a very negative effect on their net worth because the expenses of people in comparable jobs are similar, regardless of their sex. Consider this illustration: A tuna sandwich costs Ms. Jones, an account supervisor, $3 at the deli; it also costs Mr. Smith, an account supervisor, $3. But Mr. Smith earns $25,000 a year and Ms. Jones earns $15,000. Now suppose that by some arcane money magic, their salaries were equalized, but the menu at the deli now read, "Tuna Sandwich: Men—$3; Women —$5," and that those price differentials were applied to all expenses from housing to vacations in Aruba. The effect would be exactly the same as the present salary discrimination.

If you're a woman, face this fact: You have the same financial needs and responsibilities as a man, but you have a much better chance of spending part of your life, especially your old age, in poverty—unless you do something about it yourself. Don't count on the government or even your husband. If your job pays too little, get another job in a company that rewards skills and not gender. If you must learn new skills, do so.

Other people who may have insufficient incomes are those who are either undereducated or who lack technical skills. It is unfortunate that so many college students major in such subjects as history, English literature, and classical studies, then graduate into a world that demands engineers, computer programmers, and accountants.

If you are in this position, you have two options. One is to learn to be satisfied with less income—and for many people who truly love certain jobs more than income, that's fine. The other is to get technical training and qualify for higher-paying positions. You may find you can enjoy great literature or think philosophical thoughts much better when you have a good income than you can when you're poor.

Too Much Expense

Most people's financial problems involve too much expense, not too little income. Money you earn can be put into one of three places: into an expense that makes no contribution to your net worth, such as rent, food, entertainment, clothing, or auto insurance; into an expense that makes some, but little, contribution to net worth, such as jewelry, collectibles, or a car; or into an investment that contributes completely to your net worth, such as high-yield certificates of deposit, mutual fund shares, wisely-chosen common stocks, or real estate. How you allocated your resources in the past determined what your present net worth is; how you allocate your resources from now on determines what it will be one week, ninety days, and even years in the future.

THE GERMANS' LAWS OF FINANCIAL FITNESS ☐

- When people are young, they look for the pot of gold at the end of the rainbow; as they get older, often all they have is the pot.
- When you add up your assets, you will have less than you hoped for.
- Everything always costs more than you expected.

Ten Fast Remedies for Money Headaches
(one week)

MONEY HEADACHES have a lot in common with physical headaches—in fact, money headaches often cause the physical kind. You can take two aspirin and lie down to get rid of physical headaches, but the treatment isn't quite so simple for the money kind. However, money headaches can be cured by facing the problem; rooting out the cause; and taking immediate corrective action.

TOO MUCH MONTH FOR YOUR MONEY— THE PROBLEM

In the 1960s, a popular Osborne cartoon showed a man nervously chewing a pencil and looking at a calendar. The caption read, "Too much month left at the end of your money?" The situation is real enough for many people, and it's the most common cause for money headaches.

The symptoms. In most cases, a salary that refuses to stretch from payday to payday doesn't indicate insufficient income; it means that the timing of expenses with the arrival of paychecks is off. If you have this problem, you would probably be just fine if you had one extra paycheck to help you get caught up. Except for the fact that the boss isn't likely to give you an extra paycheck, and also that you'd soon spend a little extra here and there until you again had month left over when the paycheck ran out.

The cause. Obviously, the underlying cause of this

problem is a lack of money management. Everyone hates to budget, but, at the least, you should learn to spend as carefully the week after payday as you do the week before, instead of spending while you have it and starving when you don't, with no spacing in between.

TAKING ACTION—THE SOLUTION

You need to take three financial aspirin—a drastic reduction in expenses and a money windfall for immediate relief, followed by a long-term cure in the form of realistic money management.

You can go on a financial diet, but how can you get a windfall? Don't bet on the horses or play the state lottery, because you're almost certain to lose—then you'll have even less money. In case you haven't realized it, the lotteries are designed to get your money, but they give precious little back. On the average, the states pay back about 50 cents on every dollar they take in. A slot machine in Las Vegas pays back 80 cents; a blackjack table pays back about 95 cents. State sponsorship gives the lotteries an aura of respectability, yet the National Council on Compulsive Gambling estimates that 10 percent of the players are addicts.

In 1983, *The Wall Street Journal* cited a woman who bet $10 a week on the New Jersey lottery as saying, "It's a good investment. If I could hit the lotto game, I could retire at 22." In fact, the odds against her are 3.2 million to 1 per ticket. And buying more tickets or buying over a longer period of time doesn't change the odds. So here's a realistic look at what the young woman is doing. She's giving the state $520 a year in additional, optional taxes. If she saved that $520 a year in an Individual Retirement Account at 10 percent interest compounded annually, in 30 years she'd have $89,896, with the odds 100 to 1 in her favor. As it is, the odds are 3.2 million to

1 that she'll end up without a penny left of the $15,600 she will have gambled away. Yet every person who sells lottery tickets can tell you of case after case in which people who live on welfare waste their precious dollars trying to strike it rich.

Ten Fast Remedies

Here are ten practical steps to consider instead:

1. *Go on a real money diet for just enough time to get caught up.* This means eating brown-bag lunches, sticking strictly to beer-and-TV dates, walking to work, not buying any new clothes, and so on. Practice austerity, austerity, austerity. This method hurts, but for most people, it's the surest way to get an immediate increase in cash. And, just as though you were on a low-calorie weight-loss diet, everyone will feel sorry for you and envy your willpower at the same time. Just don't let others pick up the check too often or they'll resent it.

2. *Cut your losses and eliminate any single major drain on your resources.* This is the toughest medicine in this book, but it works. For example, Sue and Tony sold a van they had wanted for years because it was keeping them broke with upkeep. Harry and Janet sold a house that was simply too much for their budget. In each case, the couple found they could get by with, respectively, a car and an apartment until they earned more money.

3. *Contact your most pressing creditors at once.* If *you* call *them*, it will probably shock them into being agreeable; they are used to dunning people, not being called. Tell them you have temporary problems and need relief. Specifically, suggest one or more of these steps: refinancing your debt so that payments are extended, but lowered; paying only interest for a few months until you can get caught up; or, best of all, skipping a few payments with interest accruing. If your cred-

itors adamantly disagree, politely suggest that there is always personal bankruptcy. This may help to persuade them, because they would probably rather wait a little longer for payment in full than get only a fractional payment.

4. *Put on a bill-payer loan, but mean it.* Use the proceeds *only* to pay overdue bills, then don't borrow again. The danger with bill-payer loans is that many people use them to get caught up; then, when the financial stress eases, they immediately get behind again. Only now, they have the bill-payer loan due in addition to their other debts.

5. *Check your life insurance to see if you have any cash value you can borrow.* Remember that policy you really didn't want but bought from an old college dorm buddy? If it's more than a few years old, you may have some cash value you can tap through a policy loan. Or perhaps you should switch any whole life to term insurance and take your surrender value in cash.

6. *Sell that stamp (or some other) collection.* Almost everyone has some items around the house that other people would pay to have. Perhaps it's an old comic book or two, or Frankie Laine singing "Mule Train" on an unscratched 78 rpm record. But don't underprice your items. Check to see what the market value is. Some people may be willing to pay a great deal for your junk —er, collectibles.

7. *Hold a tag or garage sale* if you own many items that aren't collectibles, but are useful. Lump your junk —er, unneeded property—together and sell it all at once. Even if you've been amassing such things for only a few years, it's not hard to raise anywhere from $500 to $1,000 at a tag sale. And here's a tip—try to coordinate a combined sale with your immediate neighbors. You'll get proportionately larger crowds, and the competition will actually improve sales in most cases. Here's another tip—use the money you get for financial relief, not for buying stuff at other people's tag sales.

8. *Use a holiday bonus gift or a legacy to get caught up rather than to splurge.* At Christmastime, it's tempting to blow that bonus; when you make that unexpected sale, a new car can look awfully good; when Aunt Hattie dies, it's more fun to buy a new wardrobe than to pay old bills. But nothing can liven up your incoming mail as much as an absence of late notices for unpaid bills.

9. *Do a quick extra job.* Perhaps you can do a bit of freelance consulting. Or sell a skill. If you're an accountant, why not moonlight and do some tax work? As a teacher, you could do a bit of tutoring. Whatever you do for a living, you can almost certainly do a little extra of it for a short time to earn that needed money.

10. *Put a hobby to work.* If you tie trout flies, start selling some; if you're a really good baker, start selling special cakes. Almost everyone is good at something that can produce extra cash.

None of the above remedies for your financial headaches is easy. They all require effort and sacrifice. But they do work.

THE GERMANS' LAWS ON MONEY HEADACHES □

- You can get rid of money headaches by cutting off your head, but that's a little drastic.
- Often, the problem is, when you're rich, it's on paper; when you're broke, it involves cash.
- You can help a money headache by realizing that the less money you have, the more there is for you to get.

Debt—Get Out of the Red and into the Pink
(two weeks)

WITH ANY EFFECTIVE FITNESS PROGRAM, you must begin by finding out if you really are out of shape, just how out of shape you happen to be, and why you're out of shape. After that, you can take steps for immediate relief and long-term recovery.

YOUR DEBT CONDITION

How can you tell when you're too much in the red? Here's a quiz that will help you. For each statement, give yourself 3 points if your answer is "always"; for "often," 2 points; for "sometimes," 1 point; and for "never," 0 points. Write the number of points in the space provided after each statement.

Debt Condition Quiz

1. I can't make it through the month without overdrawing my checking account.   —
2. My checkbook balance gets a little lower every month.   —
3. I pay the minimum due (or less!) on my credit and charge cards each month.   —
4. I am behind on one or more installment payments due.   —
5. I am at or near the borrowing limit for my credit cards and/or charge cards.   —

6. I don't have a savings account, or, I do, but it's
    dwindling.   —
7. I get by each month by counting on income
    from overtime or odd jobs.   —
8. I borrow to pay anticipated bills, such as taxes
    or insurance premiums.   —
9. I use credit cards to pay for necessities and/or
    to get cash advances to live on.   —
10. I don't know exactly how much I owe.   —
11. I juggle my bill payments, paying one creditor
    this month, another next month.   —
12. I get dunning letters or phone calls.   —
13. I sell or hock valued belongings in order to
    pay my bills.   —
14. I worry about my bills and/or have family
    disputes over money.   —
15. Money troubles make me feel physically ill.   —
    Now add up the points to determine your
        score and write the number in the space at
        the right   —

Find your score below and see how you rate:

0: Check in at the nearest cathedral for your halo.
You're a saint!

1–15: You're above average and doing well, unless
all of your points added up in answer to just four or five
questions. If this is the case, score yourself again—you
fudged on some of the answers.

16–30: You're average, but you can do better if you
try. Mostly, realize that using a credit card isn't "paying
with plastic." It's paying, eventually, with your own
hard-earned cash.

30–45: Be careful—you're on dangerous ground.
Your credit health could slip into terminal status if you
don't practice some immediate financial preventive
medicine.

45–60: Are you not sleeping very well? Or worse, are you sleeping just fine because you can block out your troubles? In either case, you're in bad shape, and you'd better do something, now! This book can show you how.

HOW OUT-OF-SHAPE ARE YOU?

How much credit use is too much? When does borrowing become excessive and painful? The following table can help you quickly determine your personal credit spending fitness. To use it, you'll need your checkbook stubs or register and a pencil and paper.

Credit Spending Fitness Table

MONTHLY TAKE-HOME PAY	AMOUNT YOU SPEND PER MONTH IN INSTALLMENT PAYMENTS (WITH CREDIT HEALTH RATING)			
	Excellent	Good	Fair	Poor
$ 850	$ 85 (or under)	$105	$130	$ 170 (or more)
900	90	115	135	180
1,000	100	125	150	200
1,250	125	155	190	250
1,500	150	190	225	300
1,750	175	220	265	350
2,000	200	250	300	400
2,250	225	280	335	450
2,500	250	315	375	500
2,750	275	345	415	550
3,000	300	375	450	600
3,500	350	440	525	700
4,000	400	500	600	800
4,500	450	565	675	900
5,000	500	625	750	1,000
5,500	550	690	825	1,100
6,000	600	750	900	1,200

From the stubs or register, add up all of the monthly installment payments you made during the last six months. Include credit-card payments, except for those made in full within the interest-free period; auto loan payments; charge account time payments; personal loan payments; and so on. *Important:* Do *not* include home mortgage loan payments. Now divide the total by six, and you'll have the average amount you spend each month for installment payments.

Next, figure out your monthly income after taxes. Find the amount nearest to your take-home pay in the first column, then read across until you find the amount nearest to what you spend monthly in installment payments. Your credit health rating will be listed at the top of that column.

If your rating is "Excellent" or "Good," great. If you still don't have enough cash to go around, the problem isn't too much credit spending, it's too much spent on something else—housing, food, insurance, entertainment, or whatever. You don't need to spend less on credit, you need to spend less, period.

If your rating is "Fair," be careful. You're getting by, but you're marginal. An unexpected illness, accident, or financial need could flatten you because you have no credit reserves.

If your rating is "Poor," chances are you have the late-notice blues or phone-collector headaches. You might even be tempted to bang your head against the wall until it hurts so much that you don't notice your other troubles. Or you might decide to down six double martinis in rapid succession, which will soon help you forget the pain. However, in either case you won't be treating the *cause* or *causes* of your financial headaches, but merely prolonging the agony.

WHY ARE YOU OUT OF SHAPE?

If you're out of shape, it may be because overuse of credit has hurt you. Here's why:

Like some people, *you may act as though loans are payable in Monopoly money*—they're strictly for fun, and the bills never really come due. You may have forgotten that, although credit cards are just plastic, the debts they incur must be repaid with real dollars. As a result, you may not realize just how costly credit is. *Credit cards are really loans on which substantial interest is charged,* despite the clever ads that some banks and stores run stressing their shopping, dining, and travel convenience. A survey conducted by *The Wall Street Journal* during the 1984 Christmas shopping season showed that, while bank and credit union annual interest charges on personal loans averaged 15.5 to 18 percent, those on credit cards averaged 17 to 22.25 percent. Credit cards should be used for safety and convenience, not for borrowing.

The table on the following page will help give you an idea of what credit can cost. Use the average monthly installment payment that you calculated for the Credit Spending Fitness Table. Find that amount in column 1, then look in column 2 to find the approximate amount you pay in finance charges each year.

As you can see, the amount you spend on finance charges adds about 10 percent per year to the cost of the goods and services you charge. In addition, this chart generously assumes a new car payment at a low rate, so if there is no such thing in your calculations, your real costs will be a bit higher. The point is if you spend $500 a month in installment payments and your take-home pay is $30,000 a year (which puts you into the "Poor" category), you're paying about $600 a year, or more than

Annual Financing Cost Estimator

Average Monthly Installment Payments	Annual Financing Costs
$ 100	$ 121
150	182
200	240
250	300
300	361
350	421
400	481
450	541
500	601
600	721
700	841
800	962
900	1,082
1,000	1,202

one week's income, just for the privilege of paying in installments. And to put that into perspective, realize that $600 will buy you an acceptable new stereo; two to five nice jackets; a round-trip, three-day vacation; or a pedigreed dog.

Because of the cost of credit, *the goods and services you charge or borrow to buy cost a higher proportion of your income than you'd planned to spend.* Thus, if you budget 6 percent of your income for clothing, but charge all of your clothes, you'll actually spend not 6 percent, but 6.6 percent. In dollars, that means, if you earn $25,000 per year after taxes, instead of spending $1,500 per year on clothes, you'll effectively spend $1,650. That extra $150 a year could buy you a little nicer lunch every day at work instead of making your bank richer.

Excessive credit spending keeps you from taking advantage of cash discounts and from gaining the advantages of dealing from a cash position. Yes, it is illegal for merchants to discriminate against credit purchasers by giving cash discounts, but many still do it. You can dicker with cash in hand, and you'll often win. In addition, dealing with cash in hand means increasing your strength. Don't believe it? Try paying for something with a $100 bill some day and see the respect you get. Perhaps the merchant or service provider is knocking down on his income tax and welcomes cash, or perhaps he just impresses easily; either way, cash works, especially in larger denominations.

HOW TO SPELL RELIEF

Now you should know if you're really out of shape, how bad the problem is, and why it exists. So what can you do about it? If you're subject to pain from overdue bills, here's how to start getting well.

Use first-aid to put your creditors on hold. If the late notices and dunning calls are coming, start with a deep breath and try to relax. Here are the facts: Under the Fair Credit Reporting Act, a collector may *not:*

- Dun you with embarrassing tactics; in other words, he can't drive up in a van lettered "We Collect from Deadbeats" or shout at your door.
- Tell your friends, neighbors, or co-workers about the debt in any way.
- Abuse you on the phone, tie up your phone, or impugn your character to others on the phone. This means he can't say to someone else who answers your phone, "Is So-and-So in? This is the Hardnosed Collection Agency calling about the overdue Jones Department Store account."
- Physically threaten you or your property; that's assault, a criminal offense.

· Nonphysically threaten you or your property; if the threat contains a demand for payment, that's extortion.
· Use mailings that look "official" (in many states).

What a collector *can* do is *collect legally* and, if necessary, through the courts.

But why not apply first-aid to end the problem? If you're annoyingly in the red, end the pain by arranging to start ending your debts.

First, fill in the work sheet below, listing all your debts and the amount you can reasonably expect to pay each month to each creditor and the date when you will be able to pay.

Creditor Work Sheet

Creditor	Total Due	Amount Overdue	Amount I Can Afford Monthly	Date I Can Make First Payment
_____	$____.__	$____.__	$____.__	__/__/__
_____	$____.__	$____.__	$____.__	__/__/__
_____	$____.__	$____.__	$____.__	__/__/__
_____	$____.__	$____.__	$____.__	__/__/__
_____	$____.__	$____.__	$____.__	__/__/__
_____	$____.__	$____.__	$____.__	__/__/__
_____	$____.__	$____.__	$____.__	__/__/__
_____	$____.__	$____.__	$____.__	__/__/__
_____	$____.__	$____.__	$____.__	__/__/__

Next, phone or visit each creditor. Explain why you can't pay. Creditors are human, too, and if you have problems—including having gotten carried away with spending—they'll probably understand. Then ask for an extension and—this is most important—get an agreement on the amount you will pay each month and the date on which you will make the payment. Send a letter of confirmation to each creditor; make sure you keep a copy for your files. Or have each creditor sign a copy of your letter to indicate agreement. Realize, however, that, by sending the letters, you are acknowledging your debts and making a commitment to pay.

What happens if the creditors won't go along with you? Above all, be pleasant—you don't want legal troubles. But realize you can apply pressure, too. You can always imply that if you don't get another chance, you may have to file for personal bankruptcy, in which case they'll really have to wait and will really lose money. Or they can give you a break and get paid in full by waiting a little while. Smile as you give each creditor the choice, and you'll probably get that other chance.

This plan should stop the calls and letters at once. You've stopped the bleeding, as it were, now start healing the wound by first stopping credit spending immediately. Lock up your credit and charge cards or give them to a trusted friend to hold for you. As a last resort, destroy them or return them to the issuers. Second, you should meet each of your adjusted payments as they come due, otherwise your creditors may get angry and call off the whole revised deal.

Some people are in deeper trouble than this, however, and personal bankruptcy is a very real choice for about 450,000 of them a year. But before going that far, there are three other outs:

See a professional debt counselor. Seek out a member agency of the National Foundation for Consumer Credit. If you can't find one in the Yellow Pages, get the address of the one nearest you by writing to the Foundation at 8710 Georgia Avenue, Silver Spring, MD 20910.

The debt counselor will get a complete financial picture; recommend any government or charitable agencies that may help—if, for example, illness is a factor; help plan a budget; and make a list of all debts, then contact all creditors to arrange an acceptable payoff schedule. There is no charge for this service, except a $5- to $10-a-month fee for postage and paperwork. Best of all, the dunning will stop.

File for debt reorganization under Chapter 13. This section of the Bankruptcy Reform Act of 1978 is sometimes known as the "wage earner plan" and is available to anyone who is badly in debt and has a regular income. If you are in this situation, here's what to do:

First, find an attorney who handles Chapter 13 cases. Ask your local bar association for a recommendation. The association will probably give you a list of attorneys from which to choose. Call several of those on the list. Ask about fees and check their record of successes. Choose an attorney with whom you feel you can work.

Give your attorney the information needed to make a list of debts and prepare a payment plan that will be filed with a bankruptcy judge. Creditors are then stopped from proceeding against you. If the plan is approved, turn over money each month to an appointed trustee, who will in turn pay off your creditors.

You may file Chapter 13 if you owe less than $100,000 in unsecured debts and less than $350,000 in secured debts. Unsecured debts include such things as credit-card balances and personal loans that have been given on the strength of your signature. Secured debts are those for which you have pledged collateral. A car title to cover an auto loan or equity in your home for any of various types of loans, such as a home repair loan, is considered security for a debt.

File under Chapter 7 of the Bankruptcy Reform Act. This is the real thing—voluntary personal bankruptcy. This wipes out your debts when you are *really* in the red. Again, you should see an attorney who specializes in such cases. You may *not* file for personal bankruptcy if you:

- Have more assets than liabilities, even if you can't quickly sell the assets
- Have obligations primarily secured by the items purchased, such as cars or boats
- Had a discharge in bankruptcy within the past six years
- Had a Chapter 13 plan that paid less than 70 cents on each dollar owed during the past six years
- Have a cosigner on some of your debts
- Lied on a credit application

Under the new amendments to the Bankruptcy Reform Act, which were approved on June 29, 1984, you may *not:*

- File Chapter 7 if you have sufficient income to cover necessities plus a part of your obligations
- Keep household possessions in excess of $4,000 in value
- Cancel debts used to purchase luxury items within 40 days of filing or loans of $1,000 or more made within 20 days of filing

But you may:

- Keep equity in a home not to exceed $7,500 for singles and $15,000 for a married couple
- Keep jewelry valued up to $500 and a car worth up to $1,200

Personal bankruptcy hurts, but if you're desperate, it can save your financial life.

THE GERMANS' LAWS FOR GETTING OUT
OF THE RED

- People who can least afford to borrow, borrow.
- "Them that has, gets"; "them that gets, gets more."
- When you borrow, it's Monopoly money; when you pay it back, it's real.

The Healthful Way to Use Credit Cards
(thirty days)

YEARS AGO, religious extremists called playing cards "the devil's pasteboards." If they defined holding a poker hand as an occasion of sin, what would they have called the possession of a modern wallet bulging with charge and credit cards?

Just as playing cards can be misused by compulsive gamblers, so credit and charge cards can be misused by compulsive spenders. In both cases, the end result can be a financial cancer that may be terminal in its effects. If Chapter 3 showed that you're in the red, chances are credit-card misuse put you there.

A FEW DEFINITIONS

Credit cards are issued by banks and sometimes by oil companies. They may be used to get credit in a number of business establishments and even, in some cases, to obtain cash advances against your account. Normally, there is a modest fee for credit-card use, typically ranging from $15 to $25 a year. In addition, interest is charged on the unpaid balance of your bill, usually at the rate of 1.5 percent per month. This interest is for any amount not paid within the interest-free grace period.

Charge cards are issued by retail stores and may be used only to charge purchases made in the issuing store. There is no annual fee, but interest on the unpaid balance is usually charged at rates similar to those for credit cards.

Debit cards are issued by banks to allow customers to have direct access to their checking or savings accounts. There is usually no annual fee. Debit cards may operate automatic teller machines or, rarely, point-of-sale terminals in retail stores. A credit card may double as a debit card with the addition of a magnetic strip to activate a computer.

Smart cards are popular in parts of Europe and are just starting to be used in the United States. They are credit/debit cards impregnated with a computer microchip that keeps a transaction record right in the card—sort of a modern-day version of the old-fashioned passbook.

HOW CREDIT CARDS CAN WORK FOR AND AGAINST YOU

Credit, charge, and debit cards are great financial facilitators. They get things done—and fast. Want to rent a car? Just try to do it without a credit card. Afraid of muggers in the city? Carry a bank card for your night on the town. Want absolutely iron-clad proof of purchase for tax purposes? Use a credit or charge card and pay the bill by check. See a bargain but have no cash? Buy the item at once by charging it. Short on cash on Sunday night? Stop at the bank's automatic teller machine and tap your account for $100.

Unfortunately, credit, charge, and debit cards can deplete your assets faster than any financial tool ever designed. Credit and charge cards make it too easy to borrow; debit cards make it too easy to withdraw money from the bank; and all of them make it too easy for you to be ripped off by crooks if you don't carefully check your statements for accuracy.

"It's just Monopoly money," Jim laughed as he picked up the $200 dinner check for himself, his wife, and four friends. But it wasn't Monopoly money a month later when the bill came in. Jim earns $25,000 a year, which, after taxes, is about $10 an hour. So Jim had to work 20 hours to pay that one bill. No one sweats for 20 hours to pay a bill in Monopoly money!

"Wow!" Mary said, as she eyed a great dress on sale. "It's beautiful, and a steal at $125!" And it was, but Mary didn't need it. Nevertheless, she could easily say, "Charge it, please." Mary earns $15,000 a year, so based on her take-home pay, the dress cost her almost 21 hours of work time.

Remember the old gags about the Easy Loan Company? It gave credit to everyone, charged high interest rates, and always collected in the end. In those days, bankers would ask loan applicants, "Why do you want the money?" and they often tried to talk people out of borrowing if repayment seemed difficult. Nowadays, your friendly banker has brought the Easy Loan Company to you through the credit card and the automatic overdraft checking account—which usually just increases your credit-card balance by the amount of any overdraft loan. You can borrow now for anything and pay back just a few dollars a month, seemingly forever. But you *will* pay back or you'll be in deep trouble. You may even lose the home whose equity you unwittingly pledged as collateral.

PSYCHOLOGY

A credit or charge card makes everyone rich—for the moment. With a credit card and a line of credit of $2,000, Joe, a postal clerk who earns $18,000 a year, can be just as big a spender as Pete, the surgeon who earns $180,000 a year. However, when the bills come due, Pete has 10 times the resources with which to make payment.

Without a credit card, this fact is always apparent. If there were no such thing as credit cards, Pete would probably carry quite a large bankroll. Joe would not. Pete could see a fancy new stereo in a shop window, plunk down $1,800 in cash, and not miss it. He would, after all, be spending only 1 percent of his annual income. If Joe did the same thing, he would agonize first, because $1,800 would be a whopping 10 percent of his annual income. One thousand dollars to Pete is equal to $100 to Joe.

For the most part, people are careful about how they spend cash because they can physically see it dwindle. The same is true when they write checks because they can see their balances decline as they fill in their check registers.

But people are careless with credit and charge cards, and even with debit cards to some degree. This is because they don't see how quickly their assets melt away, and they ignore that melting in a number of ways.

First, people count on future income. Then many of them will spend that same anticipated income tax refund, to use a common example, four or five times. Second, people hope for a miracle before the day of reckoning. A state lottery payoff, perhaps. Third, people know that, as a last resort, they can let the balance create a loan and opt for minimum monthly payments.

HOW MUCH DOES A CREDIT CARD COST?

You know your annual bank credit-card fee. It's probably about $20 a year per card. But do you know your interest rates? They vary. In some states, they're very high. That's why some big-city banks, for example, have their credit-card operations in South Dakota or Delaware, where there is no set interest ceiling. So some banks operating from other states are charging as much as 23 percent per year instead of the 15 to 18 percent to which most states limit them.

The following table shows how much a credit card can cost per year in finance charges. The table is for various amounts of credit repaid in installments over a one-year period.

Yearly Credit-Card Costs

MONTHLY PAYMENT	ANNUAL FINANCE CHARGE WITH INTEREST CHARGED AT:		
	15%	18%	23%
$ 50	$ 49.85	$ 60.10	$ 77.22
75	74.79	90.14	115.83
100	99.72	120.19	154.44
150	149.58	180.29	231.66
200	199.44	240.38	308.88
250	249.29	300.48	386.10
300	299.16	360.58	463.32
350	349.02	420.67	540.54
400	398.88	480.77	617.76
450	448.73	540.86	694.98
500	498.58	600.96	772.20

Question: Given the information in the table, why do you think some banks with millions—yes, millions—of credit-card accounts want to operate their card business from states where they can charge higher rates?

Corollary question: Don't you think you should shop for the best deal in annual fees as well as the best deal in rates?

Further question: In fact, why pay credit-card finance charges at all?

Realize for a moment just what a dollar means to you. As you know, it is simply the basic unit of exchange in our society—you receive a dollar for doing so much work; you spend a dollar to get so much in goods or services. If you work for the minimum wage, a dollar represents about 18 minutes of work; if you are a psychiatrist earning $120 an hour, a dollar represents about a half a minute of work. As a result, a person earning $120 an hour (that amounts to about $240,000 a year) won't think twice about spending $5 because, to that person, $5 represents two-and-a-half minutes of work. To the person earning $3.35 an hour, $5 represents an hour and a half of work.

The following table will demonstate the cost of credit-card interest in terms of working time, assuming that the item listed is charged and then paid for in installments. An annual interest rate of 18 percent is assumed; it is also assumed that the hypothetical people in the examples work a 40-hour week, 50 weeks per year.

The Work-Time Cost of Interest

INTEREST COST IN WORK HOURS, BEFORE TAXES, TO CHARGE:	ANNUAL INCOME			
	$12,000	$25,000	$50,000	$75,000
$5 gloves	9 mins.	4.3 mins.	2.2 mins.	1.4 mins.
$25 purse	45 mins.	21.6 mins.	10.8 mins.	7.2 mins.
$35 hat	63 mins.	30.2 mins.	15.1 mins.	10.1 mins.
$50 shoes	90 mins.	43.2 mins.	21.6 mins.	14.4 mins.
$125 dress	225 mins.	108.0 mins.	54.0 mins.	36.0 mins.

The point is, the lower your income, the higher your relative interest costs are in terms of hours of work. If a woman who earns $12,000 a year uses a credit card to buy the entire outfit in the above table, she would, before taxes, have to pay the interest costs with 7.2 hours of work. A woman who earns $75,000 a year and buys the outfit would only have to work about 1.15 hours to pay the interest costs. Realize how many work hours credit-card interest payments will cost *you*.

Nonetheless, using a credit card can sometimes save you money, even if you pay in installments. If there is a sale with real bargains, paying interest can be worth it. For example, if you buy a sofa that sells for $600 for 20 percent off (that's a price of $480), and you pay for it in installments, you will pay $86.40 in interest. With the $120 off, you will get a net saving of $33.60.

You must realistically weigh the advantages and disadvantages of charging a purchase in order to use credit healthfully.

Further Dangers

About 50 percent of those who use bank-issued credit cards—certainly the most common type of plastic money—pay their bills as they come in. Thus, for them, the cards are simply a convenience. They incur no finance charges and pay only a modest annual fee for the safety of not having to carry cash. But the other 50 percent pay their balances on an installment basis and often keep their outstanding balances right up to the authorized limit.

Moreover, when people do make regular payments, banks *almost always increase the credit limit*. So the person who lives up to that limit is almost certain to get into financial difficulty, eventually. Should a real emergency arise, there would be no credit reserve to tap with a personal or other loan. Even if this doesn't happen, this person will add tremendously to his or her cost of living by adding finance charges to the cost of the goods and services charged to the cards.

THE REMEDY

Use your credit cards to your advantage, not to that of the lender. If you're behind at the moment, stop using your cards at once. Then, if possible, pay your outstanding balances off at once, or at least as quickly as possible. And from then on, pay your bills within the 30-day interest-free period. If you have no such period (and a few banks and other lenders do charge interest right away), switch to another card issuer.

Easier said than done? Of course. But look at all of the people who run for miles every day to protect their hearts, who avoid saccharine to prevent cancer, and who painfully quit smoking to avoid heart trouble, lung disorders, and various kinds of malignancies. Giving up an addiction is never easy, but it can be done. And, oh, how free you'll feel when those balances drop to and stay at zero!

THE GERMANS' LAWS OF CREDIT-CARD USE ☐

· Worry is the interest paid by those who borrow trouble.
· When credit is too easy to get, it's also too easy to use.
· You can beat the system. Your banker won't love you, but then, do you plan to marry your banker?

Expenses—Lose Your Financial Flab
(thirty days)

AS ANY DIET DOCTOR will tell you, there is only one cause for obesity—eating too much. Some people do it with trencherman meals; others do it by constantly nibbling on tidbits. Either way, the calories add up. Expenses add up in exactly the same way.

If you're suffering from financial flab, you have one of two problems or a combination of the two. Either you spend too much on your large expenses, you dime yourself to death on the little ones, or you do both.

If you need to get rid of financially fat expenses, the first expenses to consider are the big ones, specifically the costs for your housing, insurance, and automobile.

Some people spend far too much on these items, trying to impress salespeople and refusing to ask questions they feel may make them appear to be "dumb" or "cheap."

The following guidelines can help you to shed flab in some important areas.

HOUSING COSTS

You should limit your housing costs—including utilities, maintenance, and insurance—to no more than about 30 percent of your gross income. Here's how that works out: Check back to Chapter 1 for the total of your last year's adjusted gross income plus any amount saved in a retirement plan. Find that figure in column 1 of the table below. The maximum amount you should spend each month on housing appears in column 2.

Maximum Housing Cost Estimator

ADJUSTED GROSS INCOME PLUS RETIREMENT SAVINGS	MAXIMUM SENSIBLE MONTHLY HOUSING COSTS	
	Married	Single
$10,000	$ 250	$ 200
15,000	375	300
20,000	500	400
25,000	625	500
30,000	750	600
35,000	875	700
40,000	1,000	800
45,000	1,125	900
50,000	1,250	1,000
55,000	1,375	1,100
60,000	1,500	1,200

Are there any exceptions to the rule? Sure. If you don't drink, date, entertain, or go to restaurants often, and delight almost solely in your home, then you can spend a higher percentage on it. But if you lead an active social life, you may need to spend even less than 30 percent on housing to make up for it. As the table indicates, if you're single, you'll probably spend less on housing and more on credit buying and entertaining.

Of course, regional adjustments should also be made. If you live in Boston or New York, for example, you can add about 10 percent to the figures; for Sun Belt cities, subtract 10 percent; for rural areas, subtract 15 to 20 percent.

Here are some ways to save money on housing:

1. *If absolutely necessary, move to a less expensive*

home or apartment. Sometimes you can move to a nicer home that is located in a less expensive area.

2. **Reduce your property insurance costs.** It's important to have homeowner's or tenant's insurance coverage against all risks, including theft; but you can make a big reduction in premiums by taking the maximum deductible and by installing an alarm system.

3. **If you're a homeowner, reduce your property taxes.** Check on personal exemptions for being a veteran or a certain age, having a particular illness, and so forth. Make sure your property is fairly assessed in relation to other properties in your town, and file a complaint if it isn't. If you can save just $200 a year through an abatement, that will total an impressive $1,000 in five years.

4. **Rewrite your mortgage.** If you can shave 2 percent from your rate on a 30-year mortgage, you'll save about 16 cents in finance charges per month per $100 borrowed. If that doesn't sound like much, consider that a rate two points lower results in savings of $96 per month on a $60,000 mortgage.

The table on the following page shows how much you can reduce housing costs by lowering property insurance costs, cutting taxes, and reducing mortgage costs. These figures are not carved in stone; each makes a different assumption. For example, the mortgage savings figure assumes a 20 percent down payment.

The point is, if you haven't already made every attempt to trim expenses, you can probably eliminate a lot of financial flab when it comes to housing costs.

INSURANCE COSTS

If you're typical, you pay the equivalent of approximately one month's salary before taxes for insurance premiums every year. Here are some examples:

Possible Monthly Housing Cost Reductions

Original Cost of House	Insurance Savings	Tax Savings	2% Lower Mortgage Rate Savings	Total
$ 30,000	$10	$12	$ 39	$ 61
40,000	13	17	51	81
50,000	17	21	64	102
60,000	20	25	77	122
70,000	23	29	90	142
80,000	27	33	102	162
90,000	30	38	115	183
100,000	33	42	128	203

- Life insurance, $50,000 death benefit, whole life, purchased at age 35—$1,000 per year
- Health insurance, major medical—$2,500 a year, of which you pay half and your employer pays half
- Automobile insurance, $250,000/$500,000 coverage —$1,000 a year
- Homeowner's/tenant's insurance—$700 a year
- Total—$3,950 a year in premiums

If you earn $47,400 a year, those are average payments. If you earn less, you're paying proportionately above average.

Here's the way to reduce your insurance bite:

1. *Switch that $50,000 whole life policy to term insurance* and invest the amount you save. Or consider a new variable policy with an investment feature. You can save up to $800 a year.

2. *Switch your health insurance to a health maintenance organization (HMO)* and save about $300 a year. Better yet, switch to an employer who pays the entire amount. Your savings in this case? In the neighborhood of $1,250 a year.

3. *Switch to $100,000/$300,000 auto insurance cov-*

erage and buy a $1 million personal liability umbrella rider under your homeowner's/tenant's coverage to make up the difference. In addition, go for maximum deductibles on collision and comprehensive coverage. The possible savings amount to as much as $200 a year.

4. *Switch to the maximum deductible for your homeowner's/tenant's coverage.* And, as suggested before, consider installing a burglar alarm system. Even with the cost of the personal liability rider, you'll still save at least $150 a year.

Under the above alternate plan, your yearly savings could total $1,450. Make that $2,400 if you switch to an employer who pays all of your heath insurance premiums. And if your agent can't save you any money, get a new agent.

AUTOMOBILE COSTS

To save money on your car:

1. *Make sure you have a vehicle you can afford.* If you have one that costs more than 15 percent of your take-home pay to maintain and operate, sell it and buy a less costly vehicle. A good used car can save you a fortune.

2. *Learn a bit of basic maintenance.* If you can do a tune-up, you'll save at least $150 a year. If you only add your own oil, you'll save about $1 a quart. If you use the self-service gas pump, you'll save about a nickel a gallon, or $30 to $40 a year.

YOUR SPENDING HABITS

If, instead of big-ticket waste, you're being dimed to death with expenses, here's a sure-fire diet that will help:

1. *Stop using credit cards except for gasoline pur-*

chases. Leave your bank cards, charge cards, and travel and entertainment cards at home.

2. *Carry only enough cash each day to meet your anticipated needs.* If the food isn't in the cupboard or refrigerator, you can't eat it. If there's no money in your wallet, you can't spend it.

3. *Leave your checkbook at home.*

Now work on your other spending habits:

4. *If you smoke, quit.* Think of the advantages. For every pack a day you smoke, you'll save about $350 a year. You will also substantially lower your risk of developing cancer and having a heart attack; you will lower your life and fire insurance premiums; and your breath will no longer smell like an unwashed barbecue pit.

5. *Try to shop sales.* With a little effort, you can save at least 10 percent on many expenditures. Keep in mind the psychology that merchants use when a sale is held —if they can get you into the store to take advantage of a bargain, they have a good chance of selling you something else at full price. So buy just what you intended, period. And don't buy something you won't really use just because it is being sold at a low price. Also, keep in mind that some sales are rigged. An old trick is to raise the price of an item for a day or two, then advertise it as marked down for a so-called "sale price" that is pretty much the same as the regular price. Still, if you shop carefully, sales can save you money. See the chart "When Items Go on Sale" for the months when merchants usually lower prices on specific items.

6. *Whenever possible, drop to the next lower grade in the products you use.* Buy the special chain-store or generic brand products at the supermarket; switch from French to California wines, from unleaded premium to unleaded regular gasoline.

When Items Go on Sale

ITEM	LIKELY TO BE ON SALE IN
Appliances	January, July
Bedding	January, February, August
Books	January
Cars, new	August, September
Cars, used	February, November
Clothing, summer	June, July
Clothing, winter	November, December
Linens	January, May
School supplies	August, October
Televisions	May, June
Toys	January, February

7. *Eat fewer restaurant meals.* The average American spends 37 percent of his or her food budget in restaurants, and the typical restaurant meal is at least double the price of the same meal prepared at home. If you're typical, you spend about 18 percent of your take-home pay on food each year, or about 6.7 percent in restaurants. Thus, for each $1,000 of your take-home pay, you probably spend about $67. This means that if you earn $20,000 a year after taxes and cut your eating out in half, you'll save almost $700 a year.

8. *Don't buy state lottery tickets.* They are an insidious form of taxation that you can avoid. If you're a regular player, you can save up to $250 a year or more.

The point is, by cutting back the big expenses as well as the nickel-and-dime ones, you can get rid of your financial flab. And while you can get started in just 30 days of concentrated effort, the good effects will continue to accrue for a lifetime.

THE GERMANS' LAWS ON LOSING
FINANCIAL FLAB

- Everything that's fun is either fattening, immoral, or expensive.
- No matter how hard you shop for an item, the day after you buy it, it will go on sale.
- Studies prove that the best time to buy anything was last year.

Build Your Money Muscle
(two weeks)

IT HURTS to get shoved around, especially when the shoving is financial. Sticks and stones may break your bones, but a financial beating can break your spirit. Consider these examples:

Case One: Ellen is a hospital dietitian who lives alone. She is always careful to pay her bills at once, yet when she calls the plumber, she may wait for weeks to get service. Her neighbor, Bill, is an accountant. He pays his bills when they're due, but not instantly; yet when he calls the plumber, he gets service at once, often within the hour. Ellen feels furiously helpless. Why is she financially weaker?

Case Two: Henry wants a loan for $2,000; so does his friend, Pete. Both have the same income; both have marginal credit ratings. Henry gets stalled; Pete gets immediate approval. Why?

Case Three: Mary is a manager at Klaustrophobic Kitchens, Inc. She has 10 years on the job and earns $15,000 a year. Jim, who works for the same company, is also a manager with 10 years seniority. He earns $25,000 a year. Why the different salary levels?

Here are some of the answers:

Case One: As a female, Ellen was trained to be a "good girl," which meant, among other things, paying bills not just on time, but as soon as they're received. As a result, her promptness doesn't impress the plumber one bit—he expects it. (By the way, she is also used to being made to wait in line; Bill isn't.) Ellen has a psychological problem that causes her to project an image of financial weakness.

Case Two: Pete got the loan because he flexed his money muscles. When he made his application, he acted as though he expected the loan to be approved. He exuded confidence in his own future, his ability and intention to repay. Henry, on the other hand, was negative. Of course, he didn't say, "Maybe I won't be able to repay," but his lack of self-confidence said it for him. It's the old story of the partially filled bottle of wine—Pete's is half full, Henry's is half empty. The difference in attitude was enough to make the loan interviewer believe in Pete. Henry finally got his loan, but only after a wait and a struggle. Like Ellen, he has a psychological problem that results in an image of financial weakness.

Case Three: Mary is being discriminated against because she is a woman. She knows that women earn about 60 cents for every dollar earned by men in comparable jobs. What's more, her boss knows it. He's delighted to pay her less than he pays Jim, and she's willing to accept less. Mary is financially weak because she has been conditioned to be.

In each of the above cases, the person suffered from an image problem that resulted in financial softness. If you feel financially shoved around, realize that how others see you is almost always a reflection of how you see yourself. So when it comes to money muscles, how you see yourself largely determines what, if any, problems you may face.

WOMEN AND MONEY

The above is especially true if you are a woman, although many men suffer from the same financial weaknesses. Women who aspire to so-called "masculine" careers often avoid the negative self-image, while men who opt for jobs in the "pink-collar ghetto," as clerks, librarians, elementary school teachers, or in other traditionally "feminine" positions, suffer right along with the women.

An excellent book, *Great Expectations: The Psychology of Money* by Dr. Henry Clay Lindgren, professor of psychology at San Francisco State University, describes some amazing phenomena, proven in several noteworthy experiments. The experiments he cites showed that women paid themselves less than men paid themselves and—this is the interesting part—women also paid men less than men paid women or other men. In other words, women seem to feel that work itself is worth less than men do, regardless of who does it. Thus, many women are willing to accept less in income than men for comparable jobs. In one experiment involving college students, groups of men and women were assigned tasks and were asked to set their own pay. The women paid themselves just 80 percent of what the men paid themselves.

But the most interesting experiment Dr. Lindgren cites involved children aged 6, 9, 12, and 15. The children were assigned tasks and were allowed to pay themselves. The girls rated their work to be as competently done as that of the boys, yet the girls aged 6, 9, and 12 paid themselves 36 percent less than the boys paid themselves and—here's the kicker—the girls aged 15 gave themselves 88 percent less! That's 88 percent *less*, not 88 *of*. Said Dr. Lindgren:

Thus the tendency for women to underprice their work, in relative terms, appears to begin in childhood and becomes especially strong after puberty. It was interesting to note, however, that girls who chose activities toward the "masculine" end of the (job) lists awarded themselves significantly more pay than the other girls did.

The report concluded, "Women tend not to behave in ways that maximally benefit themselves," and ". . . such an orientation literally is costly to those persons who hold it, especially since it makes them vulnerable to exploitation by persons who have more self-serving ideas about money and work." And Dr. Lindgren himself observed, "Women may not wish their expected pay levels to reflect on their worth as persons, but in a work-oriented world they may have little choice."

HOW OTHERS SEE YOU

Your financial muscle is made up of two parts: the stereotyped image of you as part of a group, which is imparted to you by society, and the reflection of your self-image that you project to others. Say "librarian," and you create a stereotyped image. Or say "accountant," "lawyer," "retail clerk," "bank teller," or "exotic dancer," and you create other images. Often, these images are unfair. Not all female librarians wear horn-rimmed glasses and arrange their hair in tight buns; not all male engineers know, as one wit put it, "everything there is to know about everything that's boring."

Nonetheless, all of us are, to some extent, stereotyped, and this affects our financial strength. Thus, writers become romantic figures who can't handle money; doctors, father-figures who amass deserved wealth; schoolteachers, old maids who are willing to struggle on minimal salaries; and musicians, devil-may-care types who skip town on their bills and hock their instruments to buy drugs and cheap wine.

Unfair? Of course. Some years ago, one large eastern bank gave loan applicants a very subjective and secret credit rating based strictly on the stereotyping by the bank of certain types of people. The ratings were "A,"

"B," "C," and "R." "A" was for white males over age 25, with steady employment, who made a good appearance. "B" was for other males and single women. "C" was for married women who were not taking birth control pills. And "R" was a thinly disguised attempt to circumvent the anti-discrimination laws. It stood for "reggin," which, spelled backward, meant no loan.

You may overcome stereotyping if you dress and act differently from what is expected of your stereotype. Thus, if you are flamboyant enough, you may be able to offset a staid stereotyped image; or if you are conservative enough, you may even overcome a fiscally irresponsible image. Your actions can do a great deal to build your financial strength.

MONEY ATTITUDES

Your attitudes about money have a great deal to do with determining your financial clout. If you are typical, you have been filled with ideas about money that are positively mind-twisting. You may have been taught, for example, that it is good to work hard for your money, but bad to want to accumulate a lot of it. You also may have been taught that it is good to get a bargain, even if you don't need the item bought. In *The New Industrial State*, Harvard economist John Kenneth Galbraith said, "The individual serves the industrial system not by supplying it with savings and the resulting capital; he serves it by consuming its products." An economist may see it this way, but in practical terms, this attitude leads to a "garage-sale mentality," by which people buy things they don't need, then later sell at a great loss.

Finally, you may have been taught that "poor but honest" is the opposite of "filthy rich." Some religions teach the virtue of poverty, but followers sometimes take the lesson literally rather than symbolically. True poverty is not a virtue, it is a chronic condition that makes those who are poor suffer. And no one can have a higher calling than to try to make poverty obsolete. Of course, there are the honest poor, but there are also the honest well-to-do, and the dishonest poor and the dishonest rich. Honesty and dishonesty are moral choices, and to use either as an excuse for poverty or wealth is a mistake.

The point is, the things you were taught to believe about money may have hurt you deeply. You may have been taught to work, but not demand reward; to spend, not to save; and to avoid affluence even while respecting it in others. Your own psychological makeup could be working against you, and the image you project to others could make them react negatively toward you.

CHANGING YOUR ATTITUDES

If you need to build your money muscle, chances are, the best place to start is by changing your attitudes. Then, you'll need to downplay any negative stereotypes —or play up any stereotyped advantages—while projecting a positive self-image. Finally, you can add those tricks that the truly successful use to develop their financial strength. A big order? Yes, but it can be done.

Begin with this quick test, rating yourself on a scale from 0 ("absolutely not") to 10 ("emphatically yes"). A perfect score is 0; the worst possible score is 60.

Money Attitudes

1. I was raised with the ethic that I must work hard but not expect reward.   —
2. I am really exploited by my employer.   —
3. I create conditions that encourage people to use me financially.   —

4. Money controls me instead of me controlling it. __
5. I have an unrealistic attitude in terms of what money can do for me. __
6. I fail to see money as a reward I have earned for worthwhile effort. __

Total Score __

If you earned a 0, rate yourself again—you're kidding yourself. If you earned a 30 or higher, you have some attitude problems to overcome.

In terms of your income, realize what you have to sell to an employer. We all sell time, skills, or talent. Those who sell only time often get paid the least. Everyone has time to sell; a file clerk, for example, sells time. Those who sell skills get paid a lot more; skills are things you learn in some sort of educational process. A lawyer sells skills; so does an accountant or an engineer. Talent also pays well; it is something that some people are born with and is relatively rare. An actress is paid for her talent. And people who sell a combination of skill and talent often are paid the most of all. They include top surgeons, skilled trial lawyers, and best-selling novelists.

If you're just selling time, take steps to add skills to what you have to offer, and you can dramatically increase your income level. If you need a college degree but must keep working or are in a hurry, buy a copy of Dr. John Bear's *How to Get the Degree You Want*. You can get a nontraditional B.S. or B.A. in months from a perfectly reputable school. Or add technical skills. Many communities, for example, have schools that offer quick courses in various phases of computer operation, which can give you skills that will add to your earnings.

Both on the job and off, project a positive image. If you want to be successful, act successful. That doesn't mean going into debt to buy a Porsche or always picking up the tab for dinner. But try to dress like the people who are in the job level above yours; cultivate good manners; be cheerful and enthusiastic on the job. Act as though you expect respect. This was Ellen's problem with the plumber who kept her waiting; she didn't expect him to come and he sensed it. Instead of asking him, "When can you come?" she should have asked, "Can you come this afternoon, or would tomorrow morning be better?"

THE TRICKS

Here are the tricks that you can use to impress anyone from your boss to your banker with your money muscle.

1. *Build an iron-clad credit rating.* Here's how: Pay your bills on time—not early, but on time—especially to those firms that report to credit-rating bureaus, such as utility and phone companies. And make your loan payments on time, including credit-card payments. Nothing engenders respect from lenders like an A1 credit rating!

2. *Make friends with your bank manager.* Stop and chat when you go to the bank; get on a first-name basis. If you're a woman, you may want to shop for a bank office with a woman manager. Just be sure she really has some clout herself, i.e., can she make a loan without having to get approval from higher-up? Dealing with a woman is an almost sure way for another woman to avoid sexual discrimination.

3. *Do all of one type of business with one organization.* Have all of your bank accounts with one bank; buy all of your insurance from one agency; make all of your security transactions through one broker. Being a valued customer gives you real muscle.

4. *Use psychology.* Ever see Olympic weight lifters

psych themselves up and their opponents down? Act financially responsible and you'll overcome much of whatever negative stereotyping you face. For example, do you need to buy an item from a store where you'd like credit? Pay for something once in cash with $100 bills. Want that plumber to come to your house fast? Let him know that you're a pal of the bank manager. Plumbers rely on bankers to approve home fix-up loans for their customers; and if a plumber has a reputation for bad service, his customers may have trouble getting money.

You can't become completely financially strong in two weeks, but you can make a good start—good enough to make a favorable impression on many people and to stop those bullies from shoving you around.

THE GERMANS' LAWS ON MONEY MUSCLE ⬜

- When money talks, no one interrupts.
- If you give one person $10 worth of good advice and another a dollar, the one who gets the dollar will like you more.
- When handling money, most people try to be clever when they should be trying to be wise.

Trim Your Taxes
(sixty days)

Do YOU PAY too much in health-care costs? Probably. That's why your doctor is richer than you are. But you're willing to do it to stay healthy. Chances are, you also pay too much in taxes—but that doesn't add one dime to your fitness, physical or financial.

You spend about 40 percent of your on-the-job time working to pay your tax bills. So, obviously, it pays to trim your taxes. Unfortunately, you can't lower many of them—your state sales tax, for example, or the excise taxes on your phone bills, liquor purchases, or cigarettes, except to quit phoning, drinking, or smoking. But you may be able to reduce your largest tax liability—your federal income tax—and this should be your goal.

THINK DEDUCTIONS

Like it or not, you have a business partner—Uncle Sam. No matter how you make a living, he takes his cut before you get to keep a dime. How much he takes depends on how much you make. But the important thing to realize is that everyone with the same income is not taxed at an equal level. Here's what that means:

If Sally, in 1984, had a taxable income of $20,000 and used Form 1040EZ—which means she didn't itemize deductions—she paid $3,212 in federal income tax, or an effective rate of 16 percent. But if Sally had earned another $100, she would have paid not an additional $16 in taxes, but an additional $26. This is because Sally was in the 26 percent *marginal tax bracket.* The corollary is, if Sally had reduced her taxable income by $100, she would have paid $26 less.

Susan, in 1984, also had a taxable income of $20,000, but filed Form 1040. She put $2,000 into an Individual Retirement Account. Susan paid $2,697 in taxes, or an effective rate of 13.49 percent. Her deduction not only lowered her tax liability by $515, it dropped her into the 23 percent marginal tax bracket.

But Sandy went a step further. Her taxable income was also $20,000, but she filed Form 1040 along with Schedule A to itemize deductions. It cost her about $6 for a tax guide, plus one evening with a pocket calculator. She, too, deposited $2,000 into an IRA, and had deductions of another $2,000 above the zero bracket amount as well. Her taxes were $2,237, or $975 less than Sally's. Her effective tax rate was 11.19 percent, and her marginal tax bracket was only 20 percent.

Thus, you can see that you have three options. You can file a short form, take the evening off, and pay greedy Uncle Sam a lot more than you have to; you can take a big obvious deduction and save some money; or you can wrestle the IRS for every nickel and save a lot. Seventy percent of all taxpayers do not itemize deductions; they just take the zero bracket amount. You can partially beat the system by joining the 30 percent who itemize.

The "zero bracket amount" is the amount the Internal Revenue Service allows you as an automatic built-in deduction. Except for deductions made on Form 1040, only the portion of your total deductions that exceeds the zero bracket amount may be deducted. The reason is simple. This is the amount the IRS estimates you will have as total average deductions; and, rather than have to check your figures, it just allows that amount. The trick is to find legal ways to exceed the zero bracket amount. How much can you save by taking some perfectly legal steps? Using your figures from last year's tax return, as you did in Chapter 1, find your marginal tax bracket in the tables that follow.

1985 Marginal Tax Bracket Finder

FILING SINGLY[1]

Your Adjusted Gross Income	Your Marginal Tax Bracket
$ 2,390–$3,540	11%
3,540– 4,580	12%
4,580– 6,760	14%
6,760– 8,850	15%
8,850–11,240	16%
11,240–13,430	18%
13,430–15,610	20%
15,610–18,940	23%
18,940–24,460	26%
24,460–29,970	30%
29,970–35,490	34%
35,490–43,190	38%
43,190–57,550	42%
57,550–85,130	48%
over 85,130	50%

FILING JOINTLY[2]

Your Adjusted Gross Income	Your Marginal Tax Bracket
$ 3,540–$5,720	11%
5,720– 7,910	12%
7,910–12,390	14%
12,390–16,650	16%
16,650–21,020	18%
21,020–25,600	22%
25,600–31,120	25%
31,120–36,630	28%
36,630–47,670	33%
47,670–62,450	38%

62,450 – 89,090	42%
89,090–113,860	45%
113,860–169,020	49%
over 169,020	50%

FILING AS HEAD OF HOUSEHOLD[3]

Your Adjusted Gross Income	Your Marginal Tax Bracket
$ 2,390–$ 4,580	11%
4,580– 6,760	12%
6,760– 9,050	14%
9,050– 12,050	17%
12,050– 15,610	18%
15,610– 18,940	20%
18,940– 24,460	24%
24,460– 29,970	28%
29,970– 35,490	32%
35,490– 46,520	35%
46,520– 63,070	42%
63,070– 85,130	45%
85,130–112,720	48%
over 112,720	50%

[1] Your zero bracket amount is $2,390.
[2] Your zero bracket amount is $3,540.
[3] Your zero bracket amount is $2,390.

Now see how much some commonly overlooked deductions can mean to you:

Tax Saver Table

YOUR MARGINAL TAX BRACKET	HOW MUCH YOU WILL SAVE IN TAXES IF THE DEDUCTIBLE ITEM COSTS:					
	$10	$25	$50	$100	$150	$200
11%	$1.10	$ 2.75	$ 5.50	$11.00	$16.50	$22.00
12%	1.20	3.00	6.00	12.00	18.00	24.00
14%	1.40	3.50	7.00	14.00	21.00	28.00
*15%	1.50	3.75	7.50	15.00	22.50	30.00

16%	1.60	4.00	8.00	16.00	24.00	32.00
17%	1.70	4.25	8.50	17.00	25.50	34.00
18%	1.80	4.50	9.00	18.00	27.00	36.00
20%	2.00	5.00	10.00	20.00	30.00	40.00
22%	2.20	5.50	11.00	22.00	33.00	44.00
23%	2.30	5.75	11.50	23.00	34.50	46.00
24%	2.40	6.00	12.00	24.00	36.00	48.00
*25%	2.50	6.25	12.50	25.00	37.50	50.00
26%	2.60	6.50	13.00	26.00	39.00	52.00
28%	2.80	7.00	14.00	28.00	42.00	56.00
30%	3.00	7.50	15.00	30.00	45.00	60.00
32%	3.20	8.00	16.00	32.00	48.00	64.00
33%	3.30	8.25	16.50	33.00	49.50	66.00
34%	3.40	8.50	17.00	34.00	51.00	68.00
*35%	3.50	8.75	17.50	35.00	52.50	70.00
38%	3.80	9.50	19.00	38.00	57.00	76.00
42%	4.20	10.50	21.00	42.00	63.00	84.00
45%	4.50	11.25	22.50	45.00	67.50	90.00
48%	4.80	12.00	24.00	48.00	72.00	96.00
49%	4.90	12.25	24.50	49.00	73.50	98.00
50%	5.00	12.50	25.00	50.00	75.00	100.00

As you can see, "them that has" gets to keep more of it. Taking deductions pays.

Most people know they may deduct medical and dental expenses; state and local income, property, and sales taxes; home mortgage interest expenses; and charitable contributions. But there are many other legal deductions that people may not know about or may overlook. Such deductions appear on the work sheet below. In the spaces provided, write the amount you spent so far this year in each itemized category and continue to use the work sheet throughout the year, updating the amounts.

As of late 1984, the Reagan Administration had proposed major revisions in the federal income tax laws. Briefly, if passed, the 25 brackets would be reduced to three—15 percent, 25 percent, and 35 percent—and many tax credits and deductions would be eliminated. A few things, such as personal exemptions and IRA limits, would be enhanced. In the tables just above and below, the major items that would be affected are indicated with an asterisk. In general, the plan benefits the poor and the rich; little will change for most middle-income people.

Tax Deduction Work Sheet

ITEM	YOUR COST

Form 1040 deductions

*Retirement account deposit (IRA, Keogh, or SEP)	$.
Political contributions	$.
Penalty for early withdrawal of savings	$.
Alimony payments	$.
*Marital deduction for working couples	$.
Disability income exclusion	$.
Moving expenses	$.
*Credit for the elderly	$.
*Child and dependent care	$.

Schedule A deductions

Doctor, dentist, and hospital costs	$.
Cost of drugs	$.
*Cost of health insurance	$.
*State and local income tax	$.
*Property tax	$.
*Sales tax	$.
*Excise tax	$.
Home mortgage interest	$.
Points paid to get a mortgage loan	$.

*Credit-card fees and interest $.
*Loan fees and interest $.
 Insurance loan interest $.
*Major cash contributions $.
*Out-of-pocket contributions $.
                                        $.
                                        $.
                                        $.
                                        $.

*Other contributions
   (Mileage for charity @ 9 cents a
   mile) $.
   Property donations $.
 This book $.
 Safe-deposit box rental $.
 Office supplies for investment or tax
   recordkeeping $.
 Union dues $.
 Work uniforms, purchase and care $.
 Books for your job $.
 Magazines used for work $.
 Business gifts $.
 Cash shortages made good for an
   employer $.
 Education (if needed to maintain
   current job) $.
 Job hunting costs $.
*Business entertaining $.
 Brokerage fees $.
 Financial counseling fees $.
 Gambling losses to offset winnings
   (state lottery, church bingo) $.
 Investment losses $.
 Legal fees relating to income $.
        Total Deductions $.

Because different deductions get different tax treatments, the above total is a guide, but should not be used to fill in tax forms. For example, 50 percent of the total of political contributions is deductible up to a maximum of $50 for a single taxpayer or $100 for a married couple filing jointly. However, you can get a pretty good idea of your savings by writing the total below:

Total Deductions $.

Less zero bracket amount   −   .

Times marginal tax bracket   ×   .

Minimum possible tax saving $.

LEGAL TRICKS

Many tax advisors will tell you that, unless you have a home mortgage, you're probably better off using the short form and not listing deductions. But they may be wrong. Suppose Sally, in the first example at the beginning of this chapter, decided to list all of her overlooked deductions and found that she had missed:

$ 300 to her church
$ 200 in contributions to various charities
$ 30 safe-deposit box rental
$ 20 for office supplies for tax records
$ 500 for loan and credit-card interest
$ 700 state income tax
$ 80 sales taxes
$ 25 auto excise tax
$1,855 total

Her 1984 zero bracket amount was $2,300, so she was obviously better off just letting the zero bracket amount cover her. In fact, she got an extra $445 in deductions that way, right? Partly right. But how about this perfectly legal scheme:

Every other year, Sally decides not to itemize deductions, but to take the zero bracket amount. In alternate years, she makes pledges to her charities but holds payment until January 2 of the following year. She also pays her state income tax, her excise tax, and her safe-deposit box rental and buys her office supplies in that year. One year, Sally takes the zero bracket amount and pays full taxes, but defers many deductions. The next year, whenever possible, she makes two sets of many contributions and payments. In that year, she has deductions of well over the zero bracket amount; and, in her marginal tax bracket, this means Sally saves about a couple of hundred dollars in taxes.

Legal? You bet it is. And all it takes is a little time to arrange as many contributions and deductible payments as possible to fall due at year end. This way, you can let your deductions accrue to a meaningful amount every other year and take the zero bracket amount in the alternate years.

TAX SHELTERS AND DEFERRALS

There aren't many out-and-out shelters available for average people, but there are a few, notably:

- *Home ownership* You get to deduct mortgage interest, which usually has the effect of immediately kicking you past the zero bracket amount so that every subsequent deduction really counts.
- *Retirement accounts* These tax-deferral plans include Individual Retirement Accounts (IRAs), Keogh Plans, and Simplified Employee Pension (SEP) plans. The advantage to these is that amounts contributed immediately reduce the tax you pay. Also,

income earned is allowed to grow on a tax-deferred basis. See Chapter 17 for details.

· *Custodial accounts* Such accounts, for children, usually allow savings or investment income to grow tax free. See Chapter 16 for details.

· *Clifford Trusts* These trusts allow a temporary transfer of income-earning assets to a dependent, which allows the income to grow tax-free. Again, see Chapter 16.

THE GERMANS' LAWS OF TAX SAVINGS

· The less you earn, the higher percentage of income you will pay in taxes, because wealthy people know how to legally avoid paying.

· The tax collector believes that it is wrong to allow you to keep any of your income.

· The only way to beat the system is to know how the system works.

Gain a Fast $500 or More in Savings (ninety days)

WHY SAVE?

There are many ways to categorize people—thin, fat; smart, stupid; sick, healthy; poor, rich. And those who save and those who don't.

Some people are compulsive about saving. They'd rather stash money away than spend it every time. They give saving money a bad name because they've taken any fun out of it. Actually, they're not savers, they're money hoarders. But there are good reasons to build savings. They include:

- *Accumulating money so that it can be put to work* There's truth in the adage, "Them that has gets." It's because "them that has" makes money from their money.
- *Building a retirement fund* Anyone who counts on Social Security alone for a comfortable retirement is foolish. The money simply isn't there. What's more, it never will be again. Social Security will gradually become nothing more than what it was originally intended to be—a supplement to other retirement funds.
- *Having money for a rainy day* With personal loans so easy to get nowadays, saving for a rainy day is less imperative than it once was; but it still makes sense to a point. Most experts agree that everyone should have the equivalent of two to six months' gross in-

come in basic savings before embarking on any investment program. That amount is "rainy-day" savings.

- *Having money for fun* You can build savings, not just to watch the figures in the bankbook grow, but to take a dream vacation, to buy a boat, to splurge on a really classy dress, to accumulate funds to invest in the stock market. Everyone can make a list of things that they could do with savings.

In spite of the good reasons for saving, very few people do so. The United States has the lowest personal savings rate of any Western industrial country, with averages ranging from 4 to 8 percent per year of personal income. One reason for this is that Americans have been conditioned to spend. Spending boosts the economy and makes profits for industry. Saving, on the other hand, is said to be the mark of a miser. So what do you want to be, Santa Claus or Scrooge?

There is a middle ground, of course. An ideal savings goal is 10 percent of your after-tax income each year, with allowances for the fact that you may have children or other obligations that necessitate a reduction of this amount. See the Monthly Savings Goal table, which will suggest how much you might target to save each month, allowing for taxes and dependents.

GET STARTED

If you have no savings, right about now you're saying, "Great! So I'll put that amount in the bank next payday, then the next, but I'll get bored with it. I'll get discouraged, because my savings will grow so slowly that I'll just 'forget' to make a deposit or two, then I'll just quit." And you're absolutely right! Banks make a nice profit on thousands of people who open a savings account for a small amount with all the good intentions

Monthly Savings Goal

BEFORE-TAX ANNUAL INCOME	SINGLE INCOME		TWO-INCOME FAMILY		
	Number of Dependents (including you)				
	1	2	2	3	4
$15,000	$100	$ 75	$110	$ 75	$ 60
20,000	130	100	140	100	80
25,000	160	120	170	120	100
30,000	185	150	195	150	120
35,000	210	175	225	175	140
40,000	230	200	250	200	165
45,000	250	225	270	225	190
50,000	270	250	295	250	220

of saving regularly, but then stop making deposits. Most banks charge these small, inactive accounts a dollar or two a month in maintenance fees, so they are soon eaten away.

But here's an encouraging fact: If you can start saving with a big opening deposit, chances are you'll keep right on going. The question is, where are you going to get a big opening deposit? If your state has a lottery, you could enter it. But the odds are about 100,000 to 1 against a good win. You could rob a bank, but you wouldn't. Besides, you might get caught. Your rich aunt could leave you a bundle, but you probably don't have a rich aunt; or if you do, you don't want her to die anyway. Even if you do and she does, she'll probably leave the money to a homeless cat.

Following are several ways to "save" a fast $500 to $1,000, painlessly.

SAVINGS FROM TAXES

Almost 50 percent of all American taxpayers arrange the exemptions on their payroll withholding so that they get a tax refund. (The average refund check in 1984 was $600.) If you do this, in effect it is lending to Uncle Sam, your richest relative, money on which he pays no interest at all. On the other hand, if you owe him money, he charges you interest and sometimes even penalties. The people who arrange to do this treat their refund checks like found money. Often, they blow it, which is fine— saving for fun is a good reason to save. But there are two alternatives.

First, you can file a new W4 form with your employer and adjust your exemption schedule so that you don't overpay. It's actually better to underpay a bit, since there's no penalty if you prepay 80 percent of your tax liability or an amount equal to the foregoing year's total tax. If you've been getting a refund of $600 a year, increasing your exemptions to adjust the withholding to the actual tax will result in an increase in take-home pay of $50 per month.

Second, you can sign up for the bond-a-month plan through your employer or bank. Buy a $50 bond every month. In about nine years, the $600 you saved this year will be worth $1,200.

A slow way to save? Yes, it is. But you'll be saving money you're not used to getting as income, so you won't be as tempted to stop. And cashing in bonds is a bit of a pain, so that, too, will help you hold on to them. And in case you think these amounts are peanuts, realize that, after buying just one $50 bond a month for 10 years, your savings will be worth about $9,000!

ANOTHER SAVINGS PLAN

If you're typical, you have an outstanding loan, perhaps for a car or for that vacation trip you took to Aruba. In any case, you're probably paying out between $100 to $200 a month on the loan. Soon it will be paid off.

After it is, keep sending the bank a check for the same amount, only this time, instead of a loan coupon, enclose a savings deposit slip. If you're paying out $150 a month, in 90 days you'll have $450 plus a little interest.

The trick is to remember that you have been getting by without this income. Someday, you'll borrow again and will need the money for loan repayments; but in the meantime, save it.

THE INSTANT SAVINGS PLAN

If you'd like to be able to read your bankbook before you go to bed and see a balance of $1,000, $2,000, or more—starting in just a few days—here's an infallible way to do it. It's perfectly legal, and it works on the premise that people who can't bring themselves to save *can* and *will* pay their bills.

1. *Go to your bank and apply for a loan* of $1,000, $2,000, or whatever amount you'd like to see in your savings account. Arrange to pay off the loan over a one-year period. You may have to do a sales job on your banker. Bankers like people to save money slowly, slowly, through a sort of green-paper version of water torture. If he or she won't go along, and you can make the payments, switch bankers.

2. *Use the money to invest in a one-year certificate of deposit* at the same bank that gave you the loan, pledging the CD as collateral on the loan. You will pay about 3 to 5 percent per year in loan interest above what you receive on your certificate. Thus, to borrow $1,000 will cost you a net of about $30 to $50, and your loan interest will be tax deductible, lowering your cost even more. But at the end of the year, that $1,000 will still be earning interest without incurring finance charges.

3. *Make a monthly savings deposit* instead of a loan payment after the year has gone by.

4. Renew your CD each year and use the accumulated amount in your monthly savings account to buy another. By not lumping them together, you can avoid some penalties for early withdrawal should you need to get at part of your money.

This plan is an excellent way for people to get into the "thrift habit," as bankers like to call it.

FREE UP MONEY TO SAVE

The following plan could give you over $500 in savings, starting immediately, although not as cash in hand. The plan is based on the premise—discussed in Chapter 5—that you have been oversold on some basic insurance needs and that by making adjustments, you can save money. However, instead of pocketing the savings, plan to invest the money, which you have been accustomed to spending anyway.

1. Check your life insurance. Chances are better than good that you have a whole or straight life policy. If you bought it at age 25, you are probably paying about $400 to $500 a year in premiums, before so-called "dividends," for $25,000 in coverage. Call your agent and see if you can't save between $200 and $300 a year in premiums by switching to term insurance. Then, if you faithfully invest the amount you save, your earnings will more than offset the later raises in premiums that come with term insurance. An alternative is to switch to a variable-type policy with a built-in investment feature.

2. Check your auto insurance. If you have a car that is financed, your lender will insist on collision coverage. In this case, take the maximum deductible on your comprehensive coverage. If your car isn't financed and is over six years old, drop your collision coverage altogether. If it's not that old, at least take the maximum deductible. These strategies will save you about $200 a year.

3. Check your homeowner's or tenant's insurance. Take the maximum deductible and save an average of $150 or more a year in premiums.

If you're getting worried about being self-insured for all of these deductibles, realize that you may save about $650 a year in premiums by following the plan above, so you will be able to afford to pay for minor claims. Should you have a small claim, it won't go on your insurance record and raise your premiums; should you not have a claim, you—not the insurance company—will have the $650.

Finally, as suggested in Chapter 5, make the maximum personal liability on your homeowner's or tenant's policy $100,000; make your auto insurance $100,000 per individual, $300,000 per accident; *and* write a personal liability umbrella policy with a $100,000 deductible and a maximum of $1 million to cover you for big losses. You'll probably save a net of about $150, and you'll get a lot more insurance for your money.

Add your own items. Where have you been oversold and are paying too much? Where do you have big money leaks? If you can't put aside $1,000 a year by cutting out expenses that are a waste, either you aren't trying or you're already a very careful consumer.

IT WORKS

Accumulating significant savings isn't a matter of squirreling away nickels and dimes. Real savings begin by having a desire to accumulate money for good reasons, then taking the steps to make it happen.

Every savings plan in this chapter works. They've all been tried by thousands of people just like you, many of whom thought they never could save because watching savings mount by pennies is dull. They have found that once they got a running start, saving regular but small amounts makes sense.

Some people never spend change—they save it all in a big coin bank, then deposit it in hundreds of dollars; some people bank a raise instead of increasing their spending; some people bank their Christmas bonus every year; some people save at least a portion of any unexpected bonus, profit, or inheritance.

Whatever works for you, works.

THE GERMANS' LAWS OF SAVINGS [   ]

- A dollar you lend seems more valuable than a dollar you save.
- A penny saved is useless; a dollar saved is two dollars earned.
- Anyone who expects to make money on the horses is in the dogfood business.

Rx for Quick, Inexpensive Loans
(two weeks)

MANY BORROWERS spend far too much on finance charges, for three reasons. First, most people who want a loan want the money *now*. This means they often don't bother to shop for the best bargain. Second, people are frequently more concerned about whether they can afford the amount of the monthly payments rather than about the amount they will have to pay in finance charges. Third, people often are ashamed to ask for a loan.

MISCONCEPTIONS

Many people have psychological hangups when it comes to borrowing. Lenders know this, or at least sense it, and consequently sometimes use this fact to work against borrowers. So pull up a couch, make yourself comfortable, and consider the misconceptions that may be costing you money:

Misconception 1: Lenders are doing you a favor by granting you a loan.

Fact: They make a profit by lending money. The average bank, for example, has about 85 percent of its deposits out in loans. To keep this money working, it must aggressively seek out borrowers.

Misconception 2: Lending officials look down on borrowers.

Fact: A consumer loan interviewer's job is not, for the most part, among the highest paid professions. And lending officials are human. Some of them may even have reputations for being only fair credit risks themselves. And some are even a bit envious of the upscale people who make up the bulk of their borrowers—although, of course, they don't show it.

Misconception 3: A loan is a loan is a loan.

Fact: Loan rates can vary by huge margins. In a recent case, Bank A was charging 5 percent per year more than Bank B, which was located just down the street. Why? Bank A had many loans and not much available cash; Bank B was underloaned and eager.

Why do you have hangups about borrowing? Because if and when *you* lend money to anyone, it makes you nervous. To take some of your hard-earned cash and lend it out scares you. Suppose you don't get it back? And if you make the loan to a friend, suppose it embarrasses both of you so much that it affects your future relationship?

Groundless fears? Not at all. When a person cosigns a note for a friend who borrows from a commercial lender, the odds are one-in-two that the borrower will fail to repay the loan and that the cosigner will have to make it good. What do you think that does to a friendship? And considering that a professional lender makes careful credit judgments, what are the chances of a friend failing to repay an informal personal loan?

When it comes to the psychology of credit, however, you shouldn't confuse a bank or other lenders with friends who lend money to one another. First of all, a lender checks credit ratings and makes only relatively safe loans. Second, a lender has strong legal ways to collect its loans. Third, a lender is in the business of making loans and is prepared to write off a certain percentage as uncollectible—with no personal feelings involved.

Thus, when you apply for credit, you should relax.

You're not asking for a favor; you're a valuable potential customer offering to do business with a lender. You deserve and should get respect. If you don't, you should find another lender.

THE LANGUAGE OF LENDING

To understand loans of all types you should first be familiar with a few basic terms that all lenders use:

Annual percentage rate (APR) Under the truth-in-lending (TIL) provisions of the Consumer Credit Protection Act of 1968, the APR was deemed the method for computing interest rates that must be stated in all advertising. This is to avoid what used to be the common practice of stating rates in a deceptive manner.

Finance charge Under the TIL, this is the total amount in dollars charged for a loan.

Disclosure statement Again, under the TIL, this is a statement that every lender is required to give a borrower. It sets forth the terms of the loan, including the APR and the finance charge.

You have other rights under the truth-in-lending law, the most important of which is the "right of recision," which allows you to void almost any installment purchase within three days and get back all of your down payment.

HOW TO GET A QUICK LOAN

Now that you have faced the mental blocks and misconceptions that could lead you into undesirable lending relationships, here's the way to get a quick loan.

1. *Open a checking or NOW account with overdraft privileges.* The latter is preferable because it pays interest. For normal use, simply treat the account like any ordinary checking account.

2. Fill in the required one-time credit application and request a specific credit limit. Try for at least $2,000.

3. When you need money, simply write a check and overdraw the account, thereby creating an automatic loan.

The good news about an automatic overdraft account is that, should you need money, you have prior approval of a line of credit that lets you create a loan instantly. The bad news is that many people tend to stay completely or partially borrowed to their limit. If this happens to you, it means that, should an emergency arise, you may find it difficult to get more credit; it also means your finance charges will be huge. Perhaps the greatest danger of all is that you may become "loaned up." To a lender, this means you are making all of the monthly repayments you are capable of making on your income, which means no more loans. Thus, going wild on credit-card buying for nonessentials may keep you from getting a mortgage loan for a home or a loan for a new car.

Overdraft loans are excellent in emergency situations—when you are far from home and need money for car repairs or medical expenses, for example. However, despite the ads, they are too costly to use just to take advantage of an immediate bargain, unless the price of the item to be purchased is unbelievably low. Traditionally, banks charge their very top rates for this service.

HOW TO GET AN INEXPENSIVE LOAN

To save money on installment-type loans, shop around for rates and then choose the shortest term for which you can meet the monthly payments. Don't be bashful; phone several lenders and tell them you're shopping—it may get them to shave a point or two. And use the What Loans Cost table further along in this chapter to make comparisons.

Here's the way to get a really inexpensive loan, though it may take a bit of selling on your part:

1. *Arrange for a one-payment loan,* with the entire balance to come due when the loan period is up. Lenders don't like this type of loan very much, so it may take some shopping to find one; but if you have a good credit rating, you should have some clout.

2. *Figure out the amount of the monthly payments you've avoided making* by taking the total that will be due when the loan matures and dividing it by the number of months in the term of the loan.

3. *Deposit that amount every month in a savings account.*

Why does this save you money? Because you have the use of the entire sum during the term of the loan. If you repay in installments, you obviously can't have access to the money you've paid back. But with this method, should you need to use the money during the term of the loan, you can "borrow" from the funds you are accumulating in the savings account. In addition, the finance charge will be the same whether you pay monthly or all at once. But, if you pay all at once and accumulate the money to repay the loan in a simple 5.5 percent savings account, the "payments" you are depositing will earn interest to help offset your loan charges.

Here are a few examples of how that would work in practice.

How a One-Payment Loan Plus Savings Can Reduce Net Interest Cost for Each $1,000 Borrowed

	APR	Monthly Payment/ Deposit	Finance Charge	Savings Interest @ 5.5%	Net Cost	Net Rate
1-Year Term	10%	$87.92	$ 55.00	$ 33.11	$ 21.89	4.0 %
	15%	90.26	83.10	33.34	49.76	9.0 %
	20%	92.63	111.60	34.16	77.44	14.0 %
2-Year Term	10%	$46.14	$107.50	$ 66.65	$ 40.85	3.5 %
	15%	48.48	163.70	70.00	93.70	8.75%
	20%	50.89	221.50	73.52	147.98	13.6 %
3-Year Term	10%	$32.27	$161.60	$105.83	$ 55.77	3.5 %
	15%	34.66	248.00	113.31	134.69	8.3 %
	20%	37.16	337.90	121.59	216.30	13.2 %

You can save even more if you put those monthly "payments" into a higher-yielding account. For example, if you keep a balance in a money market mutual fund or a money market deposit account, which might pay 7 percent or more, you can make your net cost of borrowing even lower.

MAKING COMPARISONS

Before you go borrowing, it's important to realize just what loans typically cost. Now that you're familiar with the APR and the finance-charge concepts, you can make comparisons among different loan plans. The following chart takes several common APRs and shows the finance charges that apply for various time periods.

What Loans Cost
(total finance charge per $100 borrowed)

APR	1 Year	2 Years	3 Years	4 Years	5 Years
6%	$ 3.28	$ 6.37	$ 9.52	$12.73	$16.00
8%	4.39	8.55	12.81	17.18	21.66
10%	5.50	10.75	16.16	21.74	27.48
12%	6.62	12.98	19.57	26.40	33.47
14%	7.74	15.23	23.04	31.17	39.61
15%	8.31	16.37	24.80	33.59	42.74
16%	8.88	17.51	26.57	36.03	45.91
18%	10.02	19.82	30.15	41.00	52.36
20%	11.16	22.15	33.79	46.07	58.96
22%	12.31	24.51	37.49	51.23	65.71
23%	12.89	25.70	39.35	53.85	69.14

Here's how to use the chart:

Considering just the *rate,* if you want to borrow $1,200 for one year, the finance charge for the loan at 10 percent APR will be $66 (12 [hundreds] × $5.50). The same one-year loan at an APR of 23 percent will cost you $154.68 (12 [hundreds] × $12.89).

Another important factor is *time.* A $1,200 loan for one year at 10 percent APR will cost you $66 in finance charges; but for three years at the same 10 percent APR, your finance charges will be $193.92 (12 [hundreds] × $16.16).

Finally, if you factor in both rate *and* time, it can really make a difference. Using the same one-year loan of $1,200 at 10 percent APR, the cost, as stated before, will be $66; but if you make the loan for four years at an APR of 18 percent, your interest costs soar to $492 (12 [hundreds] × $41).

Obviously, it pays to shop around for rates and to borrow for the shortest time possible.

THE GERMANS' LAWS ON BORROWING ⬜▭

- We should always live within our income, even if we have to borrow the money to do it.
- It is easier to borrow if you don't need the money.
- No loan ever gets approved as quickly as you'd like.

A Money-Management Fitness Plan
(ninety days)

AFTER you've gotten rid of those nagging money headaches, trimmed off the financial fat, and built your money muscle, it's important to keep in shape. Basically, this means building and maintaining your financial strength on an ongoing basis. You can go to a financial planner for help, but there are three things wrong with this approach for many people. First, there are no standards for financial planners in most states, so anyone, with or without training, can hang out a shingle.

Second, financial planners can be expensive. Some charge hefty fees, with the average being about $1,200. The commissioned ones—life insurance agents and brokerage reps—tend to oversell because they earn money only from their sales. And the incompetent ones cause you to lose money. However, if you're affluent enough, you may still need advice.

Third, if you are a typical upscale, middle-income person, you may be able to do it yourself. You'll save the planner's fee and you'll increase your investment income and reduce your costs as well. If you need help, find an advisor you can trust who has your best interests at heart.

KNOW WHO YOU ARE

Here's a simple test. There are no right or wrong answers, so be totally honest. The purpose of the test is to help you find the place money plays in your life and thus help you make some basic financial decisions. Some people can read a popular financial-planning magazine, move from passbook savings into a perfectly safe money market mutual fund, but fail to sleep soundly from then on; others can blithely lose their savings in commodity options, pop a can of beer, and forget it.

But most people get upset over risk. This is proven by the fact that, in many banks, over 40 percent of the deposit base consists of passbook savings deposits. And some people keep huge sums in a checking account simply because they don't want to have the "worry" of a savings account.

The point is simple. Don't ever get into a money plan that makes you nervous. Develop the best money-management program you can that is consistent with your anxiety level. This test will help determine that level. Score yourself on each question according to a scale of 1 to 10, with 1 point representing the least upset you are or anxious you feel; 10 represents the most.

Money Anxiety Level Determination Test

1. You have just had your wallet stolen. It contained $500. How upset are you? ___

2. You just received $1,000 in cash and can't get to the bank to deposit it until tomorrow. You must keep it in your home. How anxious do you feel? ___

3. The gang at the office has started a baseball pool. The daily bet is $1. You are being pressured to join. How anxious do you feel? ___

4. A customer of yours who plays the stock market and brags about his winnings gives you a "hot tip." You take $500 from your savings and buy 10 shares of stock. How anxious do you feel? ___

5. With the money from question 4, instead of buying the stock, you buy two call option

contracts that give you the chance for higher earnings, but also for greater loss. How anxious do you feel? _____
6. You own 50 shares of IBM that you inherited from a rich aunt. Today the market is off and IBM drops by 10 points. How anxious do you feel? _____
7. Your life savings are in insured bank accounts, but you read that banks are failing at a rate of about 100 per year. How anxious do you feel? _____
8. You receive a stern letter asking for an overdue loan payment. How upset are you? _____

Total points _____

Find your score below and see how you rate:

75–80: Take your savings, buy a large Doberman pinscher and a shotgun, put the rest of your money in a fireproof cookie jar, and spend your days—and nights—watching it. Money is not a tool for you, it is an unbearable burden.

55–74: You are very anxious about money and should try to relax about it. In the meantime, your money-management tools should be insured bank deposit accounts—checking, savings, and certificates of deposit. By wisely using a mixture of these, you can get reasonably good earnings while having peace of mind. Your life insurance should be of the level-premium permanent type, such as whole or straight life; it's an awful investment, but a real sleep-at-night inducer. You should have a retirement savings plan funded through a bank, either an Individual Retirement Account, a Simplified Employee Pension plan, a 401K Plan, or a Keogh Plan.

20–54: You have a healthy attitude toward money. You are ready for a sound asset-management plan with a mix of bank accounts, mutual funds, or common stocks. You might have term life insurance and invest what you save by not having whole life. Or you might mix insurance and investments in variable life. If you have 10 or more years until retirement, have your IRA savings include growth stocks as well as income stocks, money market mutual funds, and high-yield bank CDs.

10–19: You should quit your job, get a string tie and a straw hat, and become a riverboat gambler. Who keeps money in banks? Chances are, you spend it as fast as you make it. But if you don't, you can try commodity futures, market index options, and playing the horses. Most of all, you should try to develop a healthier respect for money.

Below 10: You haven't been reading this book. You have no respect for money and waste it copiously. You don't need a money advisor, you need to look into yourself and figure out why you want to lose money.

WHERE DO YOU WANT TO GO?

Now you have an idea of your psychological approach to money. The question remains, where do you want to go from here?

Below is another work sheet. Again, rate yourself on a scale of 1 to 10, with 10 representing the highest priority you would give to each item in the list. What concerns you the most in planning your financial affairs?

Financial Goals

1. Safety of funds   —
2. Building net worth   —
3. Current income from investments   —
4. Building a retirement fund   —

5. Beating inflation   —
6. Family security   —
7. Reducing taxes   —
8. Saving for future needs   —
9. Fast access to money   —
10. Easy financial management   —

Some things simply don't work well together. Beating inflation and safety of funds, for example, often tend to offset each other because anti-inflationary investments are often the most risky. But most goals do mesh together very nicely, if you are willing to compromise a bit and try to make them work.

The preceding chapters give details on many aspects of financial fitness. But for keeping in shape, here is a summary of specific tips, depending on how you scored yourself on the above items:

· If *safety of funds* is vital to you, concentrate your savings in insured bank deposits. But do try to keep only a small reserve in a regular or passbook savings account. Invest instead in bank certificates of deposit. To take advantage of possible rate changes, you should buy short-term CDs if interest rates seem to be going up; buy long-term CDs if they seem to be falling. If you guessed wrong and they go up when you thought they wouldn't, take that "substantial penalty for early withdrawal" (it's not that substantial and it's tax-deductible anyway) if your CD has six or more months to run and if you can get an annualized rate increase of at least 2 percent.

· *Building net worth* is the best goal for most people. It means concentrating a good percentage of your investment dollars in things that will tend to show capital appreciation. A personal residence is an excellent example; so are carefully selected common stocks; so are high-yield CDs. Most important is time. It takes time to build net worth, so you're never too young to start—though you may be too old. You can't really build a great deal of net worth if you begin at age 60, unless you have an unusually high income.

· *Current income from investments* is the goal of those who have already built their net worth—retired people, especially. For most people, current income and safety usually go hand-in-hand. If you're in a 35 percent or higher marginal tax bracket, current-income investments should include tax-free bonds and, if you like risk, real estate and research-and-development projects. But for most people, current income means high-yield CDs, solid utility stocks, preferred stocks, Treasury securities, and AAA corporate bonds.

· *Building a retirement fund* is easy *if* you begin early enough and you save regularly and *if* you invest through a tax-deferred plan, such as an Individual Retirement Account, a Keogh Plan, a Simplified Employee Pension (SEP) plan, or a 401K Plan. Don't forget that the equity you are building in your home is also an important part of your retirement fund, since up to $125,000 in profit from the sale of a principal residence is tax-free on a once-in-a-lifetime basis. Above all, *don't* trust Social Security; benefits will almost certainly be drastically reduced in future years. And *don't* trust in a company retirement plan; they can go broke—only one person in seven ever collects on a company plan.

· *Beating inflation* isn't as hard as it sounds. Your investment in a home is an inflation-beater. Bank certificates of deposit and money market mutual funds tend to pay rates about 4 to 5 points above the annualized inflation rate. However, investments in common stock aren't always anti-inflationary; if inflation forces interest rates up, as often happens, the market as a whole tends to be stagnant.

· *Family security* begins with life insurance. Have enough insurance to provide your family with about 60 percent of your current income—that will give them a standard of living similar to the one they now have. Don't buy permanent life insurance—whole or straight life or endowment. But do price out a whole life policy. Then either buy low-cost term insurance and faithfully invest the difference in cost between that and the whole life plan in bank CDs, money market mutual funds, or high-grade common stock mutual funds, or buy variable life with a built-in investment feature. In a few years, you'll have substantial investment equity. In a few more years, you can reduce your insurance because you will have built so much wealth—and your investment equity will continue to grow.

· *Reducing taxes* is also easy, if you try. Naturally, take every deduction. A number of excellent paperback books with deduction lists are available, and it pays to consult one. Most important, tie your tax reduction to your retirement plan by having an IRA, Keogh Plan, 401K Plan, or Simplified Employee Pension plan account.

· *Saving for future needs* means having a regular or passbook savings account for the accumulation of funds. Everyone should have the equivalent of two to six months' gross income in savings—but only a fraction of that should be in passbook savings because of the low interest rates. The important point is to save for goals, and if it would help to have separate savings plans, then so be it. How about an IRA for retirement, a passbook account for vacation savings, a money market mutual fund for the two-to-six-months' income equivalent emergency fund, and a common stock mutual fund for college? One more tip: *Never* save through whole life insurance—the returns are almost always very low.

- *Fast access to your money* simply means having sufficient savings in assets that can be converted to cash, not real estate, stocks, or bonds. CDs can be cashed in; so can money market mutual funds. And don't forget what bankers call "reverse income," which is a fancy way of saying your creditworthiness. You can always have fast access to the money you will some-day earn through a personal loan—if you don't abuse your credit use.

- *Easy financial management* means just what it says. Avoid any system that is onerous or you won't stick with it. Use your checkbook as your recordkeeper. Once a year, see if your spending is within the parameters outlined in this chapter. For tax purposes, look at the federal tax forms you use and label a separate envelope for each line you fill in. File the appropriate income papers and receipts in each envelope throughout the year. Then, at year's end, add up the total for each envelope, including the pertinent figures from your cancelled checks. That way, you'll have all of the figures you need to do your taxes.

Keeping in shape financially requires developing a money-positive state of mind from which a simple routine of money management will follow. Above all, be businesslike in handling your financial affairs. Remember, your own financial future is of the utmost importance to you.

Following is a simple do-it-yourself plan that really works and is relatively painless. But remember, just as there is no effective weight-loss diet based on hot fudge sundaes, there is no totally work-free money-management technique.

A MONEY-MANAGEMENT PLAN THAT WORKS

The first step in setting up any financial-management plan is to know your present situation. In Chapter 1, you should have rated your financial fitness; if you didn't, go back and do it now. Does your net worth need building? If your Financial Fitness Rating from Chapter 1 was "Excellent" or "Very Good," you're doing fine. With a "Good," you may want to try to move up a step. With a "Fair" or "Poor," you'd better try hard to move up—and soon. In most cases, that means finding ways to spend less and save more.

Consider the amount you spend in the various categories of expense. This will be easy to do if you stick to a strict budget. But you probably don't. No one likes to budget because it's boring, so budgeting usually becomes a "tomorrow" kind of thing. It starts the day after the reducing diet is successful, right after a jogging program results in rosy-cheeked good health, and after a person learns to sew or to sail or to levitate. The following is not a budget—but it works. And if you would like to set one up, you can use the results as the basis for a budget.

Get out last year's checkbook, a pencil, and a pocket calculator. Using your check stubs or register and any receipts you may have, try to reconstruct your spending, filling in the spaces of the following work sheet.

You'll probably have good records for medical costs and poor ones for entertainment expenses, because people tend to keep records of medical bills for tax purposes, but don't usually save entertainment chits. Just do the best you can.

A Money-Management Work Sheet*

	Date	Amount	Date	Amount
Housing:	___/___	$_____.__	___/___	$_____.__
	___/___	$_____.__	___/___	$_____.__
	___/___	$_____.__	___/___	$_____.__
	___/___	$_____.__	___/___	$_____.__
	___/___	$_____.__	___/___	$_____.__
	___/___	$_____.__	___/___	$_____.__
	___/___	$_____.__	___/___	$_____.__
	___/___	$_____.__	___/___	$_____.__
	___/___	$_____.__	___/___	$_____.__
	___/___	$_____.__	___/___	$_____.__
	___/___	$_____.__	___/___	$_____.__
	___/___	$_____.__	___/___	$_____.__

Annual Total $_____.__

Monthly Average $_____.__

	Date	Amount	Date	Amount
Food and Alcohol:	___/___	$_____.__	___/___	$_____.__
	___/___	$_____.__	___/___	$_____.__
	___/___	$_____.__	___/___	$_____.__
	___/___	$_____.__	___/___	$_____.__
	___/___	$_____.__	___/___	$_____.__
	___/___	$_____.__	___/___	$_____.__
	___/___	$_____.__	___/___	$_____.__
	___/___	$_____.__	___/___	$_____.__
	___/___	$_____.__	___/___	$_____.__
	___/___	$_____.__	___/___	$_____.__

*Spending Analysis (Include the amounts of checks you have written, cash you have spent, and charges you have made.)

___/___ $___.___   ___/___ $___.___

___/___ $___.___   ___/___ $___.___

Annual Total　$___.___

Monthly Average　$___.___

	Date	Amount	Date	Amount
Transportation:	___/___	$___.___	___/___	$___.___
	___/___	$___.___	___/___	$___.___
	___/___	$___.___	___/___	$___.___
	___/___	$___.___	___/___	$___.___
	___/___	$___.___	___/___	$___.___
	___/___	$___.___	___/___	$___.___
	___/___	$___.___	___/___	$___.___
	___/___	$___.___	___/___	$___.___
	___/___	$___.___	___/___	$___.___
	___/___	$___.___	___/___	$___.___
	___/___	$___.___	___/___	$___.___
	___/___	$___.___	___/___	$___.___

Annual Total　$___.___

Monthly Average　$___.___

	Date	Amount	Date	Amount
Savings:	___/___	$___.___	___/___	$___.___
	___/___	$___.___	___/___	$___.___
	___/___	$___.___	___/___	$___.___
	___/___	$___.___	___/___	$___.___
	___/___	$___.___	___/___	$___.___
	___/___	$___.___	___/___	$___.___
	___/___	$___.___	___/___	$___.___
	___/___	$___.___	___/___	$___.___

___/___	$___.___	___/___	$___.___
___/___	$___.___	___/___	$___.___
___/___	$___.___	___/___	$___.___
___/___	$___.___	___/___	$___.___

Annual Total $___.___

Monthly Average $___.___

	Date	Amount	Date	Amount
Clothing:	___/___	$___.___	___/___	$___.___
	___/___	$___.___	___/___	$___.___
	___/___	$___.___	___/___	$___.___
	___/___	$___.___	___/___	$___.___
	___/___	$___.___	___/___	$___.___
	___/___	$___.___	___/___	$___.___
	___/___	$___.___	___/___	$___.___
	___/___	$___.___	___/___	$___.___
	___/___	$___.___	___/___	$___.___
	___/___	$___.___	___/___	$___.___
	___/___	$___.___	___/___	$___.___
	___/___	$___.___	___/___	$___.___

Annual Total $___.___

Monthly Average $___.___

	Date	Amount	Date	Amount
Medical:	___/___	$___.___	___/___	$___.___
	___/___	$___.___	___/___	$___.___
	___/___	$___.___	___/___	$___.___
	___/___	$___.___	___/___	$___.___
	___/___	$___.___	___/___	$___.___
	___/___	$___.___	___/___	$___.___

___/___ $_____.___   ___/___ $_____.___

___/___ $_____.___   ___/___ $_____.___

___/___ $_____.___   ___/___ $_____.___

___/___ $_____.___   ___/___ $_____.___

___/___ $_____.___   ___/___ $_____.___

___/___ $_____.___   ___/___ $_____.___

Annual Total $_____.___

Monthly Average $_____.___

	Date	Amount	Date	Amount
Entertainment:	___/___	$_____.___	___/___	$_____.___
	___/___	$_____.___	___/___	$_____.___
	___/___	$_____.___	___/___	$_____.___
	___/___	$_____.___	___/___	$_____.___
	___/___	$_____.___	___/___	$_____.___
	___/___	$_____.___	___/___	$_____.___
	___/___	$_____.___	___/___	$_____.___
	___/___	$_____.___	___/___	$_____.___
	___/___	$_____.___	___/___	$_____.___
	___/___	$_____.___	___/___	$_____.___
	___/___	$_____.___	___/___	$_____.___
	___/___	$_____.___	___/___	$_____.___

Annual Total $_____.___

Monthly Average $_____.___

	Date	Amount	Date	Amount
Personal Care:	___/___	$_____.___	___/___	$_____.___
	___/___	$_____.___	___/___	$_____.___
	___/___	$_____.___	___/___	$_____.___
	___/___	$_____.___	___/___	$_____.___

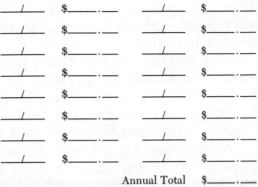

___/___	$_____.___	___/___	$_____.___
___/___	$_____.___	___/___	$_____.___
___/___	$_____.___	___/___	$_____.___
___/___	$_____.___	___/___	$_____.___
___/___	$_____.___	___/___	$_____.___
___/___	$_____.___	___/___	$_____.___
___/___	$_____.___	___/___	$_____.___
___/___	$_____.___	___/___	$_____.___

Annual Total $_____.___

Monthly Average $_____.___

	Date	Amount	Date	Amount
Other:	___/___	$_____.___	___/___	$_____.___
	___/___	$_____.___	___/___	$_____.___
	___/___	$_____.___	___/___	$_____.___
	___/___	$_____.___	___/___	$_____.___
	___/___	$_____.___	___/___	$_____.___
	___/___	$_____.___	___/___	$_____.___
	___/___	$_____.___	___/___	$_____.___
	___/___	$_____.___	___/___	$_____.___
	___/___	$_____.___	___/___	$_____.___
	___/___	$_____.___	___/___	$_____.___
	___/___	$_____.___	___/___	$_____.___
	___/___	$_____.___	___/___	$_____.___
	___/___	$_____.___	___/___	$_____.___
	___/___	$_____.___	___/___	$_____.___
	___/___	$_____.___	___/___	$_____.___

Annual Total $_____.___

Monthly Average $_____.___

Now, add up the numbers in each category and compare your totals with the numbers in the Monthly Budget Goals table below.

The Monthly Budget Goals table shows the *maximums* you should be spending (except, of course, for Savings) in each of the normally rated categories. It's based on U.S. Department of Agriculture figures, with a generous allowance for savings added in.

Now to develop a financial-management plan. For purposes of comparing, write the Monthly Budget Goal for your income range in each category in the first column of the Spending Analysis Work Sheet on page 112. In the next column, write the Monthly Average amount you spent last year. Next, adjust the Monthly Budget Goal to suit your life-style—if you don't drink, you might want to spend more on housing, for example, or if your employer gives you complete medical coverage, you can allocate most of that goal to other uses. Next, deduct your Adjusted Goal from the actual spending, or vice-versa to see where you should make adjustments.

Now you can see where your money is going versus where it should be going. And, if you're typical, Savings is probably the area where you're short.

Here comes the hard part. Where can you cut back in spending? Plan to eliminate as much overspending as possible, as indicated by your Spending Analysis Work Sheet. And in the meantime, read Part II. There, you will find financial planning tips to suit your particular life-style.

Monthly Budget Goals

CATEGORY OF EXPENSE   **FAMILY AFTER-TAX INCOME**

CATEGORY OF EXPENSE	$1,100	$1,300	$1,500	$1,700	$2,000	$2,250	$2,500	$3,000	$3,500
Housing*	$396	$468	$540	$612	$720	$810	$900	$1,080	$1,260
Food and Alcohol	198	234	270	306	360	405	450	540	630
Transportation*	187	221	255	289	340	382	425	510	595
Savings*	110	130	150	170	200	225	250	300	350
Clothing	66	78	90	102	120	135	150	180	210
Medical Costs*	44	52	60	68	80	90	100	120	140
Entertainment	44	52	60	68	80	90	100	120	140
Personal Care	22	26	30	34	40	45	50	60	70
Other*	33	39	45	51	60	68	75	90	105

* Life, health, property, and auto insurance costs are included in these items.

Spending Analysis Work Sheet

Category of Expense	Budget Goal	Monthly Average	Adjusted Goal	Difference + or −
Housing	____	____	____	____
Food and Alcohol	____	____	____	____
Transportation	____	____	____	____
Savings	____	____	____	____
Clothing	____	____	____	____
Medical Costs	____	____	____	____
Entertainment	____	____	____	____
Personal Care	____	____	____	____
Other	____	____	____	____

THE GERMANS' LAWS OF MONEY MANAGEMENT

- For some people, it's harder to manage money than it is to earn it.
- Money isn't everything in life, but having it makes everything in life more pleasant—and not having it makes everything more difficult.
- Whoever has the money makes the rules.

PART II

HOW TO STAY IN SHAPE
NOW THAT YOU'RE FINANCIALLY
STRONGER

Part I of this book deals with financial ailments that can and do plague everyone at one time or another. But there are also money problems particular to certain groups. For example:

- Women face problems because they suffer from salary discrimination.
- Men are often plagued by divorce settlements that are stacked against them.
- The courts are prejudiced against unmarried and gay couples in many money matters; and the economic deck seems to be stacked against those who live alone.
- Married couples find buying a home an almost impossible task.
- Parents face the high costs of child-raising.
- Working people are the targets of tax collectors, bill collectors, and advertisers.

Everyone has money problems that can be solved or avoided. And that's what Part II is all about.

11

For Women—
Shape Up Your Finances

JUST AS WOMEN have some physical problems that differ from those men face, they also have some financial problems that differ. These special problems exist for a number of reasons.

First, many women still have negative self-images of their financial worth. As pointed out in Chapter 6, experiments show that, from early childhood, females tend to underrate the value of their labor.

Second, our society has just recently started to come to terms with the financial potential of women. In terms of money matters, until relatively recently, women were actually classified by law with "children, cretins, and idiots." Mostly, they were not allowed to own certain property or, if they did own any, they were not permitted to dispose of it as they wished. In addition, they were barred from many types of financial transactions.

Third, women bear children. Moreover, about 50 percent of modern marriages end in divorce. In a divorce, the mother almost always gets custody of the children, along with much of the financial responsibility of child-raising.

Because of these three facts, a higher percentage of women have been and continue to be in more dire financial straits than other groups. Most Americans below the poverty line are female, either elderly widows or young unmarried women with children.

Why is all this so?

Old traditions die slowly. Even after laws are passed,

things take a long time to change. Thus, while the Equal Pay Act of 1963 requires that men and women be paid equal wages for the same work, women still earn only about 60 cents for every dollar earned by men. There are two reasons for this difference in wages. One is that some companies deliberately try to circumvent the law. Thus, until recently, a publishing firm designated some of its male employees as "circulation managers" and paid them from a base salary of $26,000, while females doing the same job, titled "circulation supervisors," were paid only $13,000. The work was identical; only the job titles and the pay differed. (Score one for the good guys—the company in effect is now out of business.) It must be pointed out, however, that this case is an exception, though not an uncommon one.

The primary reason for pay differentials between men and women is that women often seek out jobs in the pink-collar ghetto, working as receptionists, waitresses, secretaries, switchboard operators, teachers, nurses, and the like. Employers can save enormous sums simply by setting pay scales in jobs women have traditionally held below those traditionally performed by men. Usually, when men choose pink-collar jobs they suffer financially, too. Thus, nurses, secretaries, and clerks—male and female—tend to be underpaid. An exception sometimes occurs in teaching; male teachers may begin at female pay rates but often move more quickly into higher-paying administrative posts. As a corollary, when women choose jobs traditionally held by men, such as engineering, construction work, or truck driving, they tend to earn substantially more than their pink-collared sisters, although there may still be a differential between them and their male co-workers.

It is possible to be female and beat the system, but it isn't easy. In order to do so, you will have to take some of these steps:

1. *Improve your immediate financial position*
2. *Improve your financial self-image*
3. *Take steps to get a deserved increase in pay or get into a job that pays better*
4. *Be prepared for a possible divorce*
5. *Protect yourself from poverty in your old age*

IMMEDIATE FINANCIAL IMPROVEMENT

What can you do to improve your financial lot right now, in your present job, with your present skills? At the very minimum:

1. *Don't lose money.* This is the first rule of personal finance. Women are often either more conservative than men, in which case they lose investment income, or they tend to be more speculative, in which case they lose the principal invested.

2. *Establish credit in your own name, NOW.* You already have a credit record, but it may be too poor or insufficient to help you. Realize that a good payment record with the phone company is a credit reference; so is a good record of making utility payments; so is having a savings or checking account. If you've never had any loans, start with a department store charge account, add an oil company card, then apply for a bank card in your own name. If necessary, apply for a loan that is collateralized. With an auto loan, for example, the car is security for the loan—if you don't repay the loan, they take the car. Build a good credit history.

3. *Start a savings account, NOW.* Just $5 a week saved in a regular passbook account mounts up to about $265 in a year, or $1,500 in five years. And you'll get credit right away for having an account.

4. *Open a checking account in your own name, NOW.* This is a good credit reference and it gives you some instant financial clout.

5. *Increase your earnings, NOW.* You may have to ask for a raise or do some moonlighting; whatever is necessary, try to earn more.

IMPROVING YOUR FINANCIAL SELF-IMAGE

Every major classical economist from Adam Smith to Karl Marx agreed on one basic thing—the value of any product is the result of the labor required to produce that product. Admittedly, that is an oversimplification, but the essence is true. Labor produces economic value.

Why then, when tested, do girls rate the value of boys' labor higher than their own, while boys rate girls the same as themselves? Why do they also rate the value of their labor to be worth proportionately less and less as they get older? As pointed out in Chapter 6, experiments show that, if you're female, you're likely to work for less than a man, not just because that's what you're offered, but because that's probably how you rate yourself, no matter how you complain. And don't be upset with yourself for feeling this way, because that's largely how society has trained you to feel. Only be upset if you *continue* to underrate yourself.

You should improve your sense of self-worth by rating the value of your labor fairly. Now here's the tough part—be brutally honest. If you don't contribute very much to the value of the goods or services your company produces, don't expect a great deal in the way of pay. But if, after this evaluation, you feel you're not getting paid what you deserve, you should do one of two things: start taking steps to get a salary increase or a better job.

GETTING A SALARY INCREASE

Easier said than done? Of course it is, but if you're really worth more, you usually can get more. Here's what you should do:

1. *Decide how much you're worth.* Compare your pay with that of others at your company and similar companies. Check salary guides at the library.

2. *Make a list of your good points.* Concentrate on why you are profitable to your company.

3. *Ask for the raise.* If you get stalled, ask again. And again. Don't be contentious, but do be persistent.

And here's what you should *not* do:

1. *Don't threaten to quit.* You should never telegraph your punches. In other words, don't threaten, just do it!

2. *Don't be cajoled into changing your mind if you do quit.* It's possible you're just being asked to stay until a replacement can be hired.

3. *Don't complain to your fellow employees.* Such things get around, and all you'll succeed in doing is making the boss angry.

4. *Don't live in a state of anger or worry.* It is totally unproductive and only lessens your chance of success in getting a raise or finding a better job.

GETTING A BETTER-PAYING JOB

If you find the work you're doing doesn't entitle you to more pay or you can't get a deserved raise, you should find a job that pays more.

The reason some pink-collar jobs pay less than other jobs isn't always a matter of discrimination, it's often a matter of practical economics. The purpose of being in business is to make a profit. There are two ways in which a business can do so—by making sales and by producing goods and services while keeping down expenses, both of which add to the value of the products.

A salesperson sells the goods or services.

A secretary may perform valuable functions, but she contributes to neither sales nor production, so she is viewed strictly as an expense that must cost as little as possible.

A designer plans the goods to be produced; a machinist helps to produce them.

A bookkeeper neither designs nor produces goods, and thus is viewed as a cost factor rather than a profit factor.

The list could go on and on, but the point is clear. Where do you fit into the picture? If you make or sell the product or service offered by your company, chances are you're doing fairly well, with two exceptions: the service industries, such as banking, insurance, and food suppliers, which tend to use women in production jobs and still maintain low pay scales; and the government, which produces no goods and pays salaries that tend to be mediocre.

Right about now you may be saying, "But I was sold a bill of goods in school! All I can do is secretarial/food service/clerical (or whatever) work! What can I do to get into another line?"

Here are some fast answers:

1. *Consider sales.* Avoid being a store clerk, because that's a pink-collar job; and avoid being a direct distributor, such as selling cosmetics or household items to individuals in their homes, because that is also considered "women's work." But do consider executive sales. If you're any good at it, the pay is excellent. And it's a field in which women often excel and that discriminates only against those who can't sell.

2. *Try for a job that sells or produces a product.* Read the want ads for jobs usually held by men, the ads that, before anti-discrimination laws were passed, would have been headed "man wanted."

3. *Get a college degree if you lack one.* And if you have to make a living and/or raise a family while you're getting it, consider a nonresidential, nontraditional pro-

gram in which college credits are awarded for life and work experience as well as for academic courses. For hundreds of listings, pick up a copy of John Bear's *How to Get the Degree You Want.*

4. Learn a skill that pays well. Such skills include learning computer programming or repair, truck driving, and training to be a physician's assistant, a nurse practitioner, or the like.

BEING PREPARED FOR A POSSIBLE DIVORCE

Consider a typical scenario: John and Mary are young and in love. John finishes college (or learns a trade or both) while Mary works. John progresses in his career. Mary stays in an entry-level job because she wants to quit soon and have children. A child is born. Then another. John gets ahead; Mary gets bored talking to children all day. Then John gets bored with Mary. John and Mary argue. And argue. Then they get divorced. Mary is now economically on her own. She has two small children to raise and no skills. What can she do?

She can remarry, but it may be difficult for her to find a man who is willing to commit himself to a ready-made, expensive family situation. Also, Mary has been hurt and possibly isn't ready for another marriage. She can get a job, but because she lacks skills, she may earn very little; she can get a court to order John to pay child support, but unless he's rich, it might not amount to much; she can go on welfare.

Because so many of today's marriages end in divorce, Mary should realize from the beginning that her marriage may possibly end. To protect herself, she should establish financial independence. She must make sure that her banker, the people who grant retail credit, and everyone else with whom she has financial dealings know that her financial activities aren't just an extension of her husband's money-management program, but that she is responsible in her own right. She should have her own accounts and pay her own bills.

To gain her own financial base, she should have a spousal IRA with her husband and make certain that at least half, and preferably more, of the legally allowable annual deposit is made in her name. If she is younger than he, this will help her husband because the money will have a longer time to grow at interest before it must be withdrawn. Should he die before she does, she will avoid state inheritance taxes on that money, or should they divorce, she will have added financial stability for her older years.

She should also make certain she has marketable skills and should keep working while pregnant. After the baby is born, she should use a day-care center to enable her to return to work as quickly as possible.

But what if it's not newlywed Mary, but you—discovering it's too late to take these steps and facing the end of your marriage and the beginning of your financial struggles? Now you're between the traditional rock and hard place and must make some difficult choices. Here are a few tips:

1. *Don't leave anything to trust.* No matter what your ex-husband promises, get it in writing—and have your lawyer do the writing.

2. *Get a substantial agreement for child support.* Here are some discouraging facts: In 1982, 8.4 million mothers should have been receiving child support. Of that number, only 2.9 million received anything at all, and only 1.89 million received the full amount ordered by the court. A new federal child-support law, however, requires the states to adopt standards for child-support awards by October 1, 1987. And both state and federal laws are now on your side should your ex-

husband try to avoid his support payments. His federal tax refunds and, in some areas, his state tax refunds may be withheld; but with an average federal refund of $600, that won't get you very far.

3. *Try for a lump-sum payment of alimony or arrange to have an alimony trust set up.* If your former husband is affluent enough to do this and you can get a lump sum, arrange for payments from it to be annuitized, that is, paid to you to as monthly income. Either way, you will be protected should he be unable or unwilling to continue paying.

4. *Continue or begin working.* Avoid welfare (Aid to Families with Dependent Children, or AFDC) if at all possible. The degradation of being checked on by a social worker and the stigma of welfare in general adds to the burdens of raising small children and can make life miserable. It becomes a vicious cycle, nearly impossible to break.

5. *If you must go on welfare, use your time to learn a marketable skill.*

6. *Use day care to gain the time to work,* even if it means keeping just a little ahead of what welfare would pay. Work offers two advantages over welfare: self-esteem and the chance to get raises to take you above the bare subsistence level.

PREPARING FOR OLD AGE

You are responsible for your own care when you reach old age. The government won't take care of you, at least not very well. Social Security, as it has existed in the past, is going to change for the worse; you'll likely pay more in taxes and get less in benefits. If you have a husband, he might not be able to take care of you, because you'll probably outlive him; women outlive their spouses on the average of eight years. Your company pension might not do it either; fewer than one American in seven gets the pension that he or she, when young, expected to get when reaching old age.

Here are some things you can do now to prepare for taking care of yourself during your later years:

1. *Buy a home* as soon as possible if you don't already own one. The interest on the mortgage payments is tax deductible, and the value of the house will probably keep increasing. Then, on a one-time basis, when you're over 55, you can sell it and keep up to $125,000 of any capital gain totally tax-free. Or if you want to live there after you've retired, you can tap your accrued equity through a reverse annuity mortgage (RAM) to supplement your retirement income. Where available, under a typical plan, an RAM enables a homeowner whose property is increasing in value to get $200 to $500 income each month, which, upon his or her death or the sale of the property, will have to be repaid with interest plus a share of the increase in the property's value.

2. *Set up a tax-deferred annuity* if you're a teacher, nurse, or other employee of a nonprofit organization. You'll be pestered with salespeople, so you'll have plenty of plans from which to choose.

3. *Set up an Individual Retirement Account (IRA) or other qualified tax-deferred retirement plan* if you're employed. You'll get an immediate tax deduction, and the money earns income at an accelerated rate because it is untaxed until you retire. Should the need arise, you can lend yourself the IRA money for up to 60 days each year with no penalties.

4. *Set up a Keogh Plan Account* through any bank, savings association, or broker if you're self-employed. In addition to an IRA, each year, you can save up to $30,000 or 20 percent of your self-employment income, whichever is less. You deduct the amount saved from taxable income, and your balance grows rapidly because earn-

ings are compounded tax-free until you withdraw the money. Even if you have income from other sources and are self-employed on a part-time basis, but earn no more than $15,000 a year from all sources, you can save up to $750 a year or 100 percent of self-employment income, whichever is less, in a so-called Mini-Keogh Plan. If you withdraw funds from a Keogh Plan before age 59½, just as with an IRA, you not only must pay taxes on the amount withdrawn, you must pay a 10 percent penalty. However, with a Keogh Plan (but not with an IRA), you are further penalized by not being allowed to make any further deposits for five years.

THE GERMANS' LAWS OF FINANCE FOR WOMEN

- When you think you're finally getting ahead, you've overlooked something.
- Don't invest in anything that rusts, rots, or eats.
- The best way to get credit is to prove that you don't need it.

For Men—
Protect the Heart of Your Money

MEN HAVE about twice as many heart attacks as women do, at least until women reach menopause. Presumably female hormones protect women against heart disease to some extent. Two other factors work against men. Though this appears to be changing, men smoke more than women; and just about all unbiased medical experts agree that smoking causes heart attacks. Second, until recently, men experienced more job stress than women; and it's a known fact that stress can kill.

Translated into financial terms, these metaphors mean three things. First, being female somewhat protects women against financial death. True, women are economically exploited. And it is more difficult for a woman to attain financial success than it is for a man. On the other hand, it is easier for a woman to get welfare assistance, child support, or other subsistence-level aid than it is for a man. Women, it appears, have narrower financial parameters than men do; but, although men can earn money more easily than women, they can also suffer total financial collapse more easily.

Second, just as men smoke themselves into the grave more often than women, they tend to overspend themselves into financial problems more frequently. Ask any bank lending officer who is the better credit risk, all things other than gender being equal; the banker will tell you the woman is. Men tend to overspend and overborrow more often than women do.

Third, as a group, men suffer more financial stress

than women do. Women may object to this concept, but the fact is, men in our society are still expected to perform and to be good providers—failure to do so is still a stigma. If a woman fails to provide, she can blame it on discrimination, social attitudes, her children's needs, or whatever; but if a man fails, it's his fault alone. The financial stress this puts on men is enormous.

How can you, as a man, cope with these things?

SOCIAL DISCRIMINATION

Society discriminates against your maleness in two ways. Unless you are very ill, you are expected to be financially self-sufficient; and if you are married, you are usually expected to be responsible for your wife and children, even after a divorce.

Suppose you lose your job. Chances are you'll also lose all of your income. Yes, you can probably collect unemployment compensation for a while, but you'll have trouble getting welfare assistance. You probably won't want it anyway. Having been raised with the ethic that you are the provider, your pride won't allow you to accept a handout.

Should you find yourself unemployed, here are some sensible suggestions to remember:

1. *Accept your unemployment benefits.* Men who don't are foolish because unemployment benefits come from an insurance fund to which their former employers contributed on their behalf.

2. *Make a list of your financial assets and liabilities.* If you don't know where you stand now, you can't estimate the value of possible future resources.

3. *Drastically cut down spending.* Hide your credit cards from yourself.

4. *Make finding a job your primary job.* Be methodical and businesslike in your search.

The second aspect of social discrimination against men involves divorce. No matter how affluent his wife or how financially strapped he happens to be, society usually expects the husband to pay.

Consider an example: Harry and Ann were married for eight years. Harry, employed as a bank clerk, earned $15,000 a year, while Ann studied for a degree in social work. The couple have two children, ages six and seven. After Harry learned that Ann had been sleeping with a local garage mechanic, he divorced her. He desperately wanted custody of the children, but the judge awarded them to Ann. The judge also awarded the children 50 percent of Harry's after-tax income for child support. Two years later, Ann remarried. She also got her master's degree and a $25,000-a-year job. Ann now has a joint income with her second husband of $56,000 a year, plus about $8,000 a year in child support from Harry. Harry has also remarried. He and his second wife, who is pregnant and can't work, must live on his remaining $8,000 a year. Unfair? Sure, but it happens.

There are good and valid arguments for alimony and child support. For example, in the early years of a marriage, a wife still often abandons her interests in favor of those of her husband so he can further his career. When such a marriage breaks up, the wife is entitled to share in the success her husband achieved because of her help. That makes sense. What's more, no one could argue against a man's responsibilities to his children.

But realize this: should a divorce occur, no matter how civilly it started out, it is almost certain to end in bitterness. This usually starts when the couple begins to divide their accumulated assets.

Here's hoping you have a good marriage. But in case yours is one of the almost 50 percent that end in divorce, here are some steps you can take that will help to protect you and still be fair:

1. *Get a lawyer to represent your interests.* No lawyer can fairly represent both you and your wife.

2. *Try to come to a fair agreement* with the help of your attorneys. Don't rely on the courts; they almost always make the settlement one-sided in favor of the ex-wife.

3. *Consider selling your home* if you own one. An ex-wife is often given the couple's home as her part of the settlement, but this can be a mistake. For one thing, she may not be able to afford the upkeep; and should she have to sell, she would have to pay a real estate salesperson's commission, thereby reducing her assets. Don't consider any portion of the sale price that you give to your wife to be deductible as alimony. The Tax Reform Act of 1984 requires that any alimony payments that are more than $10,000 per year must continue for at least six years in order to prevent big property settlements during the first year of a divorce. The appreciated value is no longer taxable to you as a capital gain, however.

4. *Opt for paying alimony rather than child support,* if the amounts are not too disparate, since alimony payments are tax deductible but child-support payments are not. Your ex-wife may prefer to get child support, however, since she will have to pay taxes on any alimony she receives.

5. *Try to make child support a percentage of income rather than a fixed amount per month.* In this way, the kids benefit from your success, but you have some relief should you fall on hard times.

6. *Try to help your former spouse to become financially independent.* This may mean helping her to go back to school or to get a job. Either way, realize that as she prospers, you will have fewer demands made on you.

7. *Beware of tax traps.* As stated above, the Tax Re-

form Act of 1984 eliminated tax liabilities on property transfers made under a divorce settlement, but made it law that those paying alimony must make payments for at least six full years in order to get tax deductions. Here's the problem: Suppose a man agrees to pay $10,000 a year in alimony for six years. He does so for five and gets his tax deductions for those five. Then he loses his job and can't pay the $10,000 for the sixth year. Guess what happens? He loses his entire tax exemption for all six years and must pay taxes even on the money he did pay out. The best way to avoid problems is to establish an alimony trust.

OVERSPENDING

Just as men are conditioned to be providers, so are they conditioned to make an impression when it comes to money. The male peacock spreads his tail and struts; the human male sometimes becomes a big spender.

Ever hear of making a "Michigan roll" or a "Philadelphia roll"? Women seldom carried them; but men did. Both terms refer to the once-common practice of wrapping a $20 bill around a wad of $1 bills, rolling them so that the $20 bill showed. Flashing this wad in any bar made people think the showoff had a lot of money. Now that mugging is more widespread, Michigan rolls are no longer common. But men can and often do show off in other ways. If overspending tends to be a problem for you, here are a few ways you can avoid it:

1. *Buy a car you can afford.* Isn't it silly, just to make a big impression, to pledge hundreds of dollars a month for four to five years for an asset that rapidly depreciates in value?

2. *Use credit cards wisely.* Remember, they may seem like pieces of plastic, but the bills have to be paid in hard cash.

3. Don't be a big spender. Times have changed. Let others share the dinner check with you, and let your date treat you at times. No one will think any less of you if you don't always foot the bill.

STRESS

Finally, ease up on the stress that money causes by facing financial reality.

1. Be honest. How much are you earning now? How much will you really be earning in a year? In five years?

2. Make and stick to a realistic budget. Decide how much you can afford to spend now and in the immediate future. Then keep track of where your money goes, periodically reassessing your financial position.

3. Give up the role of the hunter who provides for all. Let your mate share the responsibilities of breadwinner while you share the responsibilities of homemaker. Fair's fair; if she earns part of the bread, you should help with the baking and cleaning up.

THE GERMANS' LAWS OF FINANCE FOR MEN ☐

· Pretending to be rich keeps a lot of men poor.
· Most men have two chances to get rich—slim and none.
· When you're in the chips, it's easy to be chipper.

For Unmarried Couples—
Steps to Lower Your Financial Risks

LIVING TOGETHER is a way of life for many people. More and more couples are sharing a home for some time prior to marriage. And some couples, including gays who can't legally marry, never do get married. Unfortunately for such couples, the laws of our society are geared to protect those who are married, divorced, widowed, or single without a mate.

Thus, partners in any unmarried relationship could experience severe financial problems caused by the death of a partner, relatives of either partner, a severing of the relationship, or someone who wishes to use the couple's relationship against them.

Consider these examples:

Bill and Larry were a gay couple who shared a home and a very close relationship. Had the law allowed it, they would have married. After 15 years together, Bill died without a will. Bill's family, who had never accepted his relationship with Larry, claimed all of "Bill's" property—and got it. They even forced Larry to sell the house he and Bill owned jointly and give them half of the proceeds. Substitute Mary and Ellen or Sue and John for Bill and Larry. The same problem exists.

Joe and Zelda were very much in love and decided to live together. They did everything together, including having a joint savings account to put money aside for a home they would buy when they married. Because they weren't married, their banker suggested they open an account requiring both of them to sign for withdrawals.

By the time they split up, they had saved $10,000 in the account. John was then out of work, but Zelda was earning $40,000 a year. She was angry with John, so when he asked her to cosign a withdrawal enabling him to get his share of the $10,000 in savings, she said, "I'll do it the day hell freezes over!" Zelda can, and may, hold out forever. In a divorce, John could force a division; but the law makes no provisions for unmarried couples who get "divorced."

Pete has a great apartment that he's leasing, but his landlord wants him to move so she can get more rent under a new lease with a new tenant. When Sally moves in with Pete, the landlord tells them they have to move because, under the laws of their state, cohabitation is prohibited and that by performing an illegal act, Pete has broken the lease. Can they win? Maybe, but it will cost them time and money in a court fight.

Eleanor and Rose lived together for 12 years as a lesbian couple. They shared all expenses and contributed equally to the upkeep of their home. Then they split up. Both of them love music, but who gets the baby grand for which each paid half? Worse, who gets the cat that they both adore?

If these problems haven't given you a money headache, nothing ever will!

STATE LAWS

In many parts of the country, homosexuality, cohabitation, and fornication are looked on with extreme disfavor. Here are the states with laws that might affect unmarried couples who live together:

- Cohabitation, i.e., male-female relationships that entail living together without marriage, is legally prohibited in Alabama, Alaska, Arizona, Arkansas,

Florida, Idaho, Illinois, Indiana, Kansas, Massachusetts, Michigan, Mississippi, Nebraska, New Mexico, North Carolina, South Carolina, Virginia, West Virginia, Wisconsin, and Wyoming.

· Fornication is still defined as a crime in the District of Columbia, Florida, Georgia, Hawaii, Idaho, Illinois, Indiana, Massachusetts, Michigan, North Carolina, Rhode Island, South Carolina, Utah, West Virginia, and Wisconsin.

Needless to say, it's pretty hard to live together in a sexual relationship and not cohabit or fornicate.

JOINT OWNERSHIP—SOME DEFINITIONS

Before getting into a list of financial dos and don'ts for people who live together, take a few minutes to consider some terms concerning joint ownership of property.

Right of survivorship means that the jointly-owned property passes to the survivor in case the other partner dies.

Tenancy by the entirety is restricted to married couples. This arrangement offers maximum protection to both parties; there is right of survivorship, and neither party, while living, can force the other party to dispose of property that is so owned.

Tenancy in common means that there is no right of survivorship and that either party may sell or transfer his or her interest without the permission of the other. Most property owned jointly by unmarried couples is owned as tenants in common.

Joint tenancy means that there is right of survivorship, but either party may sell his or her own share and force a legal partition.

In any case, property that unmarried partners want

to own jointly must be so titled, and the partners should be listed as joint tenants or tenants in common.

HOW TO LIVE TOGETHER FINANCIALLY

Remember that the law provides for a marriage breakup, but not for the end of a relationship. Also realize that all unmarried relationships will end, either through a breakup, marriage, or, eventually, death. Taking steps to protect your interests isn't being selfish— it's doing for yourself what the law has already done for parties to a marriage. With this in mind, consider the following advice. Much of it, by the way, is also applicable to friends who share a home.

1. *Do execute a legal agreement before you move in together* that spells out who gets what and who pays what in the event of a breakup. Do it even if you're both broke, because you may someday strike it rich. A sympathetic lawyer should handle this for you.

2. *Don't have a joint checking account,* except perhaps a small one to cover household expenses. With joint checking, either party can at any time draw out all the funds unless the account agreement specifies that two signatures are required, in which case an angry partner can hold up funds indefinitely.

3. *Don't have a joint savings account or joint investment accounts.* You run the same risks as you do with joint checking.

4. *Don't have joint credit or charge cards.* Most lenders won't allow them, but even if you can get them, it's a mistake. And don't get an additional card in your name for your partner. Should your relationship end, he or she can ruin your credit history. Also, since you must file your income taxes separately, it's easier to take interest deductions when the accounts are separate.

5. *Don't borrow jointly or cosign each other's notes.*

In either case, you are responsible for the debts of the other party. Experience has proven that when a note is cosigned, the cosigner ends up repaying the loan in over 50 percent of the cases.

6. *Do make up a detailed list of the property each person owned before the live-in relationship began.* Make two copies and have both of you sign each page of both lists. Then, as additional items are bought, add them to the list with the date of purchase, the amount spent, and the name of the owner, and have both of you initial each entry. If this seems like a distrusting way to act, again, remember that the law does not protect the property rights of unmarried couples.

7. *Don't buy a home jointly.* Have you or your partner buy the home and the other partner pay rent to the owner. To be fair, adjust the rent to reflect the tax advantage enjoyed by the "owner."

8. *Do have both parties sign the lease if you rent.* This protects both of you; should one party move out, the other won't be stuck with the entire rent obligation.

9. *Do agree in writing about who gets any pets should you and your partner break up.*

10. *Do provide for separate health insurance.* Most health insurers do not recognize an unmarried partner as a spouse for insurance purposes.

11. *Do have life insurance on both parties with the other named as beneficiary.* This protects the survivor against final-illness and burial expenses should one party die. It's amazing, but the family that may insist on its "rights" in the event of the death of one partner may also insist, "You lived with him, so you take care of him —and bury him." To get around insurance companies that may not want to issue a policy to you with your partner named as beneficiary, take out the policy with yourself as owner and with a parent named as beneficiary. After the policy is issued, switch the beneficiary to whomever you wish. And should you name your partner and then break up, realize that you can again change the beneficiary *if* you have retained ownership of the policy.

12. *Do include your partner in your will.* See that sympathetic lawyer mentioned above for this. In fact, with the proper papers, a good attorney can create almost as many safeguards for your relationship as married couples enjoy. Again, should there be a breakup, you can easily change your will to reflect your new status.

THE GERMANS' LAWS OF FINANCE FOR UNMARRIED COUPLES LIVING TOGETHER ☐

- Don't let the Moral Majority find out.
- Some couples soon discover that a love nest is for the birds.
- All too often a budding affair becomes a blooming expense.

For Single Persons—
Living without Financial Stress

HAVE YOU EVER FELT frustrated thinking that the economic world is geared to the needs and wants of married couples? Or to just couples, period?

Sure, there's the so-called marriage penalty that makes federal income taxes impact slightly more on married couples. But that's usually more than offset by the huge tax benefits of buying a home, which is far more common to married couples than to singles. And supermarkets sell items at two-for-a-discount prices; one-serving-size cans of soup cost a lot more per ounce than the two-serving size; and when the fast-food chains have a buy-one-get-one-free sale, how many single people who live alone can eat two double cheeseburgers?

Single people who live alone can be put into three categories: Those who have never married or been part of a couple who has lived together; those who are divorced; and those whose spouses or partners have died.

LIVING AS A SINGLE PERSON WHO HAS NEVER BEEN MARRIED

Such a person is most often a young man or woman who is just getting started in the world. If you are in this category, income is probably not as great a problem for you as outgo is. Here are some financial survival tips:

1. *Be concerned about your income.* Income may not seem to be as much of a problem for you as it is for couples who live together. This is because you can make

financial adjustments more easily than they. Unfortunately, you could be adapting yourself to a low income by having inadequate savings, skimping on food, and generally cutting back where you shouldn't. Try to establish the same income goals that would motivate you if you were married.

2. Control your expenses. Many single people, especially young ones, spend much of their income on luxury items, such as expensive sports cars, stereos and record collections, art collections, expensive clothes, or the like. If you do this, your other needs may eventually suffer.

3. Budget carefully. Know what you need to spend, then be sure you allocate your income accordingly.

4. Save and invest. Have some liquid funds either in bank CDs or money market mutual funds that you can tap in an emergency. After that, if you are young and risk doesn't bother you, get into growth investments. There are excellent no-load or low-load growth-type mutual funds in which you can invest through a monthly investment plan. Read the ads in *Money* magazine or in the financial pages of your Sunday paper for details. However, don't jump into schemes without checking on them. Young single people are sometimes targets for salespeople who sell risky "investments."

5. Don't buy too much life insurance. Here, again, young single people can be targets for salespeople. If you have group insurance at work, fine. If not, buy enough inexpensive term insurance to cover the cost of your burial.

6. Have adequate health insurance to cover you should illness or accident strike.

7. Have tax-deferred retirement savings. Why do this if you're young? First, because you can't count on Social Security when you retire; and at current interest rates, a dollar saved when you are 35 for retirement at age 65 will be worth 6.75 times as much as a dollar saved at age 55. Second, you don't necessarily have to use retirement savings for retirement. The biggest financial advantage enjoyed by many married couples is homeownership. An IRA can help you to buy a home because the investment income grows tax-free, which means that it multiplies at a progressive rate. If you have the savings for eight or more years at 10 percent or higher annual interest, you'll still come out ahead, even after deducting the penalty for early withdrawal and paying taxes on the amount withdrawn.

LIVING AS A DIVORCED PERSON

The divorced person who has no children to support and who has a good job simply goes back to being single —almost. In this case, the scars are psychic, not financial. But how about the man who has huge alimony or child-support payments? Or the woman who must struggle to be the single head of a household on an inadequate income?

If you're a man, budget for any support or alimony payments you have to make. Of course, these payments put you in a spot. But you have responsibility for the welfare of your children. Also, if your former wife helped you get started in a career and in so doing sacrificed her own career potential, you may have a financial responsibility to her as well. But if you try to make your payments out of what's left of your income without budgeting for them, you're going to fall behind—and everyone will suffer.

If you're a woman, be reasonable in trying to collect support or alimony payments. No matter how angry you might be with your former husband, don't try to bleed him financially. It will only hurt everyone, including you. Try to build or rebuild your career goals if you haven't been employed.

For both men and women:

1. *Try to arrange a satisfactory alimony trust* as a part of the divorce settlement, if possible. When there are enough assets to fund such a settlement, it can end problems for everyone.

2. *Don't expect to continue your former married financial lifestyle.* Divorce always hurts financially, and you will both have to cut back.

3. *Have savings to cover emergencies, as well as retirement savings.*

4. *Make sure you both have adequate insurance,* including life insurance to cover any obligations you have to your children and health insurance to protect against disaster.

5. *Have a will and keep it current.*

LIVING AS A WIDOW OR WIDOWER

Because the average woman will spend eight years as a widow, it is never too early for her to prepare for this situation. One husband, for example, has been giving his wife what he chauvinistically refers to as "widow's lessons," which include teaching his wife how to change a fuse, fix a leaky faucet, and handle the family investments. There's good reason for this. Being a widow is perhaps the most difficult situation described thus far.

The largest percentage of Americans who live below the poverty level are widows. If you are not yet a widow, and are married, begin preparing for life after the possible death of your spouse. If you aren't familiar with the particulars of the family finances, insist that you become so. Insist that your spouse have adequate life insurance. When something in the house breaks down and you don't know how to fix it, insist that your husband show you how to make minor household repairs—thousands of widows pay plumbers $20 an hour to replace 20-cent washers. Most important, be sure you have adequate financial resources to carry you through living alone.

Whether you are a man or a woman, if your spouse has already died, here's some advice that may help:

1. *Learn to live economically.* This means shopping wisely, conserving your assets, and, if you are still employed, adding to your savings.

2. *Use every resource that society provides,* from fuel assistance to food stamps, if you qualify.

3. *Keep up your health insurance.* Illness could be the biggest single expense you ever have to face.

4. *Have enough life insurance* to cover final illness and burial expenses, but don't keep yourself broke paying premiums to benefit someday heirs.

5. *Try not to live alone,* especially if you own a home. By sharing your quarters, you can augment your income and/or reduce your expenses while avoiding loneliness.

6. *Work if you can.* Even part-time work could help you tremendously.

THE GERMANS' LAWS OF FINANCE FOR PERSONS LIVING ALONE

- Marrying for money is the hard way to make a buck.
- Some people never get too old to learn new ways to lose money.
- Sometimes being single means you never had it so good—or spent it so fast.

For Married Couples—
A Money Tonic for Your Future

Now THAT you've said "I do," what if your wallet says "I won't"? That's when you need a money pepper-upper, a tonic that will put iron in your financial backbone. Most of all, it's when you need a boost to keep temporary money problems from becoming chronic cash-short ailments that can lead to a cancer in your marriage. Psychologists, psychiatrists, and others who do marriage counseling state that marital problems caused by money worries outnumber those caused by sex or in-laws by at least two-to-one.

SIX PROBLEM AREAS

Remember Sisyphus? He was the legendary king of Corinth who saw the god Zeus carry off the beautiful maiden Aegina and reported it to her father. As punishment, Zeus banished Sisyphus to Tartarus and sentenced him for eternity to roll a heavy stone to the top of a steep hill. The stone always rolls down the hill, and Sisyphus has to start over and over again. Some married couples find their money problems are similar to Sisyphus' plight—they try to do the right things, but just as problem one gets solved, another comes along and they have to start all over again.

The typical married couple faces four, occasionally five, and in some cases six major money problems, usually staggered in time periods throughout their relationship:

1. During the newlywed period, getting money to set up housekeeping can be a problem.

2. During the first five years, buying a home is often a struggle.

3. In the early years and lasting for at least 20 thereafter, raising children is a financial burden.

4. After 25 to 35 years, caring for elderly parents can be a financial problem.

5. Also during that time, having children return to the home can add to a couple's financial woes.

6. And, of course, a period of unemployment can occur anytime, with the potential of creating a real money crisis.

The following sections contain some practical tips on how to face each of these problems.

THE NEWLYWED GAME

The honeymoon is over. Now it's time to settle in as man and wife. Contrary to what comedians would have you believe, a newlywed couple does need more than a bed. They need chairs, tables, rugs, and probably a television, as well as groceries and pots and pans to cook them in—the list seems endless, and so do the bills.

The real problem lies in the fact that the couple often needs everything at once. Consider a typical case: Fritz and Amy are fresh out of college; in fact, they got married the day after graduation. They both have good jobs, earning between them almost $35,000 a year—not bad for beginners. But they need an apartment, which requires a month's rent in advance plus a security deposit, for a total of $1,500. And they need a new car, which requires a down payment of $1,000 plus monthly payments of $170. They also need new furniture, which means another $1,000 down and monthly payments of almost $300 a month. On top of that, they both need new wardrobes for their jobs, for additional monthly payments of $175. What's more, after making several trips to the discount store for odds and ends, their credit-card bills are a staggering $180 a month.

Sounds unrealistic? Not at all. The amounts involved are typical; and, after years of being broke as students, the couple really thought they could handle a little debt in order to live reasonably well. But their monthly income after taxes is about $2,000, so their loan repayments of $825 plus their rent of $750 leave them just $425 a month for food, automobile upkeep, gasoline, insurance, clothing, entertainment, medical expenses, and all of the miscellaneous items that deplete every budget. Just two modest lunches eaten out each day for an average of 21 work days a month can easily add another $100-plus to their expenses.

It's not easy, but if you're facing this kind of situation, the only way to avoid beginning a marriage deeply in debt is to hold expenses down to a manageable level. First, be sure your housing costs, including insurance and utilities, don't exceed 30 percent of your take-home pay. Second, don't allow your installment loan repayments to exceed 15 percent of your income after taxes.

Fritz and Amy in the example above should have held their rent down to $600 a month and their installment payments to $300 a month. That would have left them $1,100 for other expenses. How could they do it? By renting a less expensive apartment, buying a used car instead of a new one, and by making do with less of everything, adding to their possessions with purchases paid for in cash as their paychecks were received.

Here are some further helpful tips:

1. *Don't begin with a large debt.* But if you're already in that spot, reread Chapters 2, 3, and 4.

2. *Live within your means.* Salespeople will urge

you to buy, invest, spend, and speculate—but never to save. Life insurance is a necessity, but it's not savings, so buy what you need in low-cost term insurance. The stock market is great for investing and/or speculating, but it's not savings. You should never invest before you have substantial savings or speculate before you have substantial investments as well.

3. *Begin marriage with substantial savings,* if possible. If it's not possible, begin with common sense. Realize that how you begin can largely determine the health of your marriage.

4. *Designate the most careful and money-wise partner to handle your financial affairs.* And this doesn't necessarily mean the most parsimonious; it requires the person with the best grasp of money matters.

5. *Be ready to compromise.* Living with someone is very different from living alone, so, to achieve harmony, you must both be ready to give in on small things. Single people can afford to think primarily of themselves; partners in a relationship will need to think more often of spending for the common good.

BUYING A HOME

Every married couple should buy a home as quickly as they possibly can because a personal residence offers the best tax shelter available to the average couple. There are two good reasons. First, in its present form, Social Security cannot continue to work. Changes have already been made and will continue to be made, the net effect of which will be to raise this highly regressive tax. However, the capital gains tax deferral on the rollover of profits from the sale of a private home within a two-year period is one plum no politicians have dared to touch. Nor have they touched the one-time exemption from taxable income of up to $125,000 in profit from the sale of a private home, so this accruing equity can help make up any future shortfall in Social Security benefits.

Second, both political parties are pledged to retain the income tax deduction on mortgage interest for a personal residence, no matter what other tax loopholes may be closed. This means that the taxes paid by your friends and neighbors, through the kindly offices of the IRS, will help you and others to buy a home. For the typical young couple in the 25 percent marginal tax bracket, the tax deduction effectively:

Reduces This Mortgage Interest Rate	To This
14%	10.5%
13%	9.75%
12%	9.0%
11%	8.25%
10%	7.5%

But how do you buy a home?

1. *Set your sights low enough to make home ownership affordable.* Because home prices continue to rise, it's better to get into ownership with a smaller, less expensive home than you had hoped for than it is to rent forever while trying to save a huge down payment. In addition to the equity developed from your mortgage payments, your equity increases as home prices rise, so that, after a few years, you may use it to buy a larger home.

2. *Don't get into so-called creative financing.* That's just another way of saying "more debt." Should interest rates rise, as well they may, the creative financer could be trapped.

3. *Save as large a down payment as possible,* but don't give up all of your savings because you will cer-

tainly have some unexpected expenses. As stated in Chapter 14, one way to accumulate a down payment is with an IRA. Here's an example:

The Hendersons, who have been married for five years, are both employed and have been renting an apartment. As soon as they were married, they both opened an IRA at their bank and have since each saved $2,000 a year, the annual maximum amount allowed. At 12 percent annual interest, they have accumulated $28,915 during the five years. Taking into account the IRA tax deductions, they have together actually contributed a net of $2,680 per year, or a total of $13,400. If they had saved the same amount each year in a non-tax-deferred plan and had paid taxes at the same rate, they would have ended up with only $14,475, not $28,915. When they use part of the money for a down payment on a home, they will have to pay taxes and a penalty on the amount withdrawn. But even with the taxes and penalty, they will still come out way ahead by using the IRA as a savings tool. Legal? Sure. How does it work? The multiplier effect of compound interest simply exceeds the accruing taxes and penalty when an IRA is kept going for eight to 10 years.

RAISING CHILDREN

Any married couple that has decided to have children will probably find them to be their single biggest expense. The costs are so large that the subject warrants a separate chapter in this book—Chapter 16.

ELDERLY PARENTS

Caring for elderly parents has become a major financial problem for many people. It has been widely discussed that many of the elderly are warehoused in nursing homes, and it is true that the accompanying emotional suffering is intense and widespread. However, the plight of the couple who must face this financial dilemma is often ignored. Consider a typical example:

Bruce and Helen have been married for 30 years. During the first five years, they struggled to buy a home. Making the down payment and meeting mortgage payments really kept them strapped until salary raises came through. Then, just as their home-buying expenses became more bearable, their two children reached college age. They struggled for six years to pay for the children's education, and even ended up with a residual loan to pay. Finally, it was paid off, and, with Bruce 55 years old and Helen 53, they thought they could look forward to traveling a little and to saving for a more comfortable retirement. It was then that Helen's 80-year-old father had a stroke. Her mother, who is 79, is now becoming physically incapable of taking care of him. Helen's parents have always been the type who never saved much. As a result, Bruce and Helen have an excellent chance of having to spend from $500 to $1,000 a month to help care for Helen's folks.

For both your parents' sake and yours, how can you avoid this kind of situation?

1. *Early on, suggest strongly that both parents have IRAs* funded as fully as possible and, in addition, that the parents develop adequate savings.

2. *Ask that you be familiar with your parents' finances* if they are really financially unhealthy and if there is a chance that you may someday be responsible for them. Or offer guidance to help them on their way to financial stability. And don't wait until they've retired; do it as soon as you see that the possibility may arise.

3. *Insist that your parents have adequate health in-*

surance for their sake and yours. If they have Medicare, make sure that they also have insurance to cover the gaps.

4. *Ask your parents if they want to enroll in the American Association of Retired Persons.* They can get some excellent advice and money-saving buys through this organization. For information, write to the association at 215 Long Beach Boulevard, Long Beach, California, 90801.

If you have an immediate problem with parents who need help:

1. *Expect your parents to help themselves as much as possible.* Sometimes elderly parents *can* do something themselves to help their financial situation. They might have to sell their home and move, or use it as an income-producing asset by renting rooms or even by taking out a reverse annuity mortgage (see Chapter 17). And if they do something for themselves, they'll benefit emotionally as well as financially; nothing keeps people young like being self-reliant.

2. *Use any available state or federal aid to help.* Especially know your rights under Social Security; if a claim is denied, get a good lawyer to file an appeal.

3. *Consider setting up a Clifford Trust* for the required 10 years plus a day, or set up what Boston tax expert Alexander Bove calls a "short-cut Clifford Trust" (a short-term irrevocable trust) for a lesser time if you have substantial assets and if your parents are in trouble. With a Clifford Trust, the income rights to assets are transferred to a beneficiary for at least 10 years plus a day. Then the assets revert to you. The beneficiary gets the income on which he or she pays taxes at a low post-retirement rate, and you avoid taxes on the income altogether. With a short-term irrevocable trust, you transfer the earnings on the assets to the beneficiary for however long you wish. You then have the assets revert to your

spouse on termination of the trust or to you under your parents' wills. Unless you get a divorce, you keep the assets in the family, but get the tax advantages anyway.

4. *You may want to start an IRA to be used as an emergency fund,* if your parents are incapable of doing so themselves. Admittedly, this seems like a wild suggestion, because it could certainly hurt to put your own money into it each year, but think how that money could help if and when the need arises. And your parents should return the amount they save on taxes to you, which would lessen the pain. The savings should be accumulated strictly to help out in times of real need, of course, and should not be used for any other purpose.

THE FILLED-NEST SYNDROME

You read a lot about Mama mourning the empty nest when the chicks have grown and gone, but the real tragedy for many couples occurs when their kids, grown, educated, and in their late twenties or early-to-late thirties come back home to their parents. According to one prestigious financial planner, this represents the biggest money problem that many middle-aged Americans must face. Offspring who return to the nest often represent a financial drain at a time when their parents are saving for retirement or when they are helping to support elderly parents of their own.

The best way to avoid this problem is to teach children to be independent, for their well-being and yours. In addition, children should be encouraged to develop useful, needed skills that will allow them to be independent while they pursue their basic interests. And people can and do earn their livings in fields such as art, literature, and some of the less economically oriented social sciences, if they have a solid ground in marketable skills.

Should your children return home, remember that you owe them your help, but you don't owe them your life-style or your future. And neither do they have the right to live without working while you struggle to support both yourself and them. If you see that they can and should go back out on their own, you may want to set a date for them to leave. Tell them they should find a job and/or a separate residence. And while they are with you, have them reimburse you for a fair share of their expenses. This can initiate the feeling of independence they may need to set off on their own.

A special problem exists in the case of a daughter— or, rarely, a son—who is divorced with young children to care for. In such a situation, realize that your child may be able to make a better new beginning from the old family nest. But, at the same time, a returned child with small children can play havoc with your nerves and pocketbook. So try to help, of course, but be concerned enough to aim that help in the direction of establishing your daughter's or son's independence.

UNEMPLOYMENT

Unemployment can hit at any time, and it really hurts. If either partner loses a job, the loss of income is hard to stand, because it's just human nature for a married couple to get used to living on the income they're accustomed to receiving.

What should you do if you lose a job?

1. *Do a fast financial analysis.* What do you owe and to whom? What do you own that can be converted into cash if needed? Most of all, how long will it take to get a paycheck to replace the one that was lost?

2. *Cut back on spending, fast.* Stop using credit cards, except for gas and oil to travel while looking for work.

3. *Contact creditors, if necessary, and ask for loan extensions.*

4. *Get the whole family to help with a general belt-tightening.*

5. *Apply for every benefit for which you qualify.* Never be too proud to apply for unemployment benefits —after all, you paid for that insurance protection through your employer for years.

6. *Most of all, make finding a job a full-time job* and get back to the ranks of the employed as quickly as possible.

THE GERMANS' LAWS OF FINANCE FOR MARRIED COUPLES

- Maybe marriage is called the sea of matrimony because it's hard to keep your head above water.
- The guy who wrote "Home Sweet Home" never had to live with his in-laws.
- The trouble in some families is that the kids stop being kids, but the parents can never stop being parents.

For Parents—
Surviving Your Children's
Money Growing Pains

IF YOU THINK you've had financial headaches before, just wait until you have children! Though the financial burden is worth it, you should know what you're getting into and how you can best handle it.

There are four major areas of expense in raising a child that can have a negative impact on your financial well-being:

- *The loss of family income from the unemployment of the mother.* The amount varies among families, of course; but if Mom had been earning $20,000 a year before she got pregnant and then stays home until her child starts school, the loss in family income will total about $100,000. In addition, when she returns to the job market, she'll be rusty and will probably start in at a lower salary than she would otherwise have been making at that point.
- *The medical costs of childbirth.* Although it varies, average hospital and obstetrical costs are about $3,000, plus another $1,000 for a C section (about one in three births are now by Cesarean section).
- *The actual expenses incurred in raising a child to college age.* Costs vary here, too. Obviously, it is cheaper to raise a child on a farm than in New York City, but the current average total cost is just under $140,000.

· *The costs of postsecondary education.* College costs rise yearly. As of 1984, the cost of tuition and room and board at a prestigious private college averaged from $50,000 to $60,000 for a four-year program. The costs for state colleges varied from state to state, but in general were about half that of private schools. By the year 2000, when a child born in the early 1980s will be reaching college age, costs for the big-name private colleges will exceed $100,000.

Below is a list of total costs for a child born in 1985, assuming his or her mother stops working in a $20,000-per-year job until the youngster starts school and assuming the boy or girl goes to a state college and is self-supporting after graduation:

Loss of mother's income for an average of five years	$100,000
Birth costs	3,000
Maintenance until age 18	140,000
College	60,000
Total costs	$303,000

What can you do about this huge expense? One option is not to have children, which increasing numbers of Americans are exercising. Another is to have enough money so that the costs are not so overwhelming. Or another option is to live in penury or struggle through a lifetime of debt, a situation that can cause terrible feelings between parents and children. The fourth and most viable choice for most people is to reduce their costs while maintaining a reasonable standard of living. Following are some tips on how to do the latter.

THE LOSS OF INCOME

Over 50 percent of American mothers are in the work force today, and the number is growing. One reason is that everyone wants the good life, but most families can't get it on a single salary. Women used to quit work as soon as their pregnancies became apparent. Now they seem to work until the last minute. New mothers used to stay away from the job at least until the youngest child was six years old and in school. Now many pack the kids off to day-care centers and are back on the job in six months.

If you're planning to raise a family, you can't make up the income lost by the mother's time off from work, no matter how short the period, but you can minimize its effect by taking these steps, especially if the mother plans to stop working for an extended period of time:

1. *Avoid chance pregnancies.* Since you can't plan for the unplanned, an unexpected pregnancy can hit just when you're not financially ready.

2. *Anticipate the loss of income at least one year before it impacts.*

This means you should:

3. *Get the heaviest of your big financial burdens under control before pregnancy.* Make the down payment on a home, have your major appliances all paid for, have installment payments under control, and start an IRA.

4. *Live entirely on the husband's income for one year before the first pregnancy.* During this time, save all of the wife's income. This will do two things—get you used to living on one salary *and* provide a sound emergency fund.

CHILDBIRTH AND SET-UP COSTS

Be sure your hospital and doctor's bills are covered by health insurance. If you don't have a good plan where you work, join Blue Cross/Blue Shield or a good health maintenance organization long enough before the pregnancy so that you will be fully covered. Then be ready for some expensive start-up costs. You may need to buy everything from maternity clothes to nursery furniture to a supply of disposable diapers. Plan ahead. And have enough in extra savings to absorb expected and unexpected costs without breaking your budget.

And don't hesitate to accept equipment and clothing from relatives and friends whose kids no longer need them. A used crib, stroller, and baby clothes can save many hundreds of dollars. These things are often outgrown so quickly that they're hardly worn before they're ready to be passed on to another child.

CHILD-RAISING COSTS

Junior at age one will love a 59-cent rattle. At age 17, he will love a rattletrap that costs perhaps $1,000 to buy, $1,000 a year to keep running, and another $1,000 a year to insure.

His sister, age one, will love a $1 pacifier. By age 17, she will have required everything from expensive orthodontic treatments to ballet lessons. And by then, she will have discovered designer clothes. Expensive designer clothes.

It takes a lot of money to raise a child, and the expenses, small when the child is small, grow as he or she grows. Fortunately, this tends to keep pace with most income trends. To relieve the possible impact on family finances:

1. *Teach the child about money early.* Put the child on an allowance, not as pay for chores done, but as a training program in money management.

2. *Encourage the child to begin earning some money as early as possible.* Even small children can do simple tasks for pay.

3. *Bring the child into the family financial picture as much as possible.* Too many parents go broke, not by trying to keep up with the Joneses, but by trying to keep up with their own kids' expectations.

COLLEGE COSTS

You can cut college costs drastically if you:

1. *Try for a scholarship,* either an athletic scholarship, which isn't usually available for girls, or an academic scholarship if the child can qualify. Some college-bound kids find it easier to get several smaller and less prestigious scholarships than one large one. Ask your child's high school guidance counselor what is available in your area.

2. *Determine the child's real needs.* What kind of college should he or she attend? Depending on what the child wants, a state college might provide him or her with what he or she needs just as well as a private institution.

3. *Consider two years at a local community college.* This saves a substantial amount of money, and the education is usually more than adequate to prepare the student for acceptance into a four-year institution for his or her junior and senior years.

4. *If appropriate, encourage the child to get on a work/study program at the college to help with costs.*

5. *If appropriate, consider encouraging the child to join the ROTC or the National Guard under a college-aid program.* In both cases, scholarships are available. Even without one, the monthly income comes in handy.

6. *Avoid education loans if you can.* Such loans put a drain either on you, at a time when you should be saving for your own retirement, or on your child, at a time when he or she is just starting out and the repayments make that start even more difficult.

7. *Don't be afraid of education loans if the child wants to go to medical school.* You'll probably want to spring for the best undergraduate school for which he or she can qualify. If your son or daughter is going to be a doctor someday, he or she should be able to repay education loans without strain. However, the same is not always true for dentists and lawyers.

8. *Save for the child's education with a custodial account set up under the Uniform Gifts to Minors Act (UGMA).* This is the best plan of all. Under the UGMA, you can set up an irrevocable trust for the child, the assets of which go to the child when he or she legally becomes an adult. This means two things—you can't get the money back or use it except for necessities for the child, and the income is taxable to the child, not to you. This results in real savings in income taxes because the taxes on earnings are paid by the child, so they usually amount to very little or none at all. Any bank, thrift institution, or brokerage house can quickly set up such a program for you; you don't need a lawyer to set up a UGMA account. Because UGMA benefits may be reduced by the Reagan Administration tax proposals, check on any current limits.

9. *Take advantage of any income-producing property you may have.* In case you have to make immediate arrangements to pay for your child's college education and no scholarship is feasible, you still have two options for coming up with the money if you have income-producing assets. One is to set up a Clifford or Ten-Year Trust. As discussed in Chapter 15, under this plan you transfer the assets for at least 10 years and a day to the dependent; the child gets the income from the assets and pays taxes on that income at his or her rate, which probably means paying none at all or at least considerably less than you would.

The other option works only if you have a spouse whom you trust implicitly. Under a Clifford Trust, which is a reversionary trust, the assets return to you when the trust terminates at the end of a minimum of 10 years. But if you have a child who is of college age now, you may want to set up an irrevocable trust for a shorter period. To do this, establish a short-term irrevocable trust giving the earnings from the assets to the child for the period desired; but when the trust matures, have the assets transfer to your spouse. This way, the child gets the earnings at his or her tax rate, which is low, if taxes are even paid at all, and the assets, in effect, return to benefit your household.

See a lawyer about setting up any of these trusts. Take into consideration that there will be a tax-deductible fee of about $500. Also realize that Clifford Trusts are under attack by the Reagan Administration and may be eliminated or modified at any time.

Now take a look at the following comparison of college costs. Four options are considered: paying cash; paying with a long-term student loan at an annual percentage rate of about 9 percent interest; paying with earnings from an irrevocable trust; and paying with savings accumulated under a custodial account set up under the UGMA. In these examples, assume that the parents are in the 40 percent tax bracket and that interest on either the trust funds or the custodial account are at 10 percent per year. Further assume that the UGMA account was opened when the child was three years old. In the interests of accuracy, lost income to the parents, less a tax adjustment, was deducted from the trust earnings figures.

College Cost Comparisons

	TOTAL COSTS TO PAY COLLEGE TUITION EXPENSE OF:		
	$40,000	**$80,000**	**$100,000**
Cash	$40,000	$ 80,000	$100,000
Student Loan (10-year payback)	60,804	121,608	152,010
Irrevocable trust	36,000	72,000	90,000
UGMA account (15 years of saving)	18,000*	36,000**	45,000***

* Saving $100 per month
** Saving $200 per month
*** Saving $250 per month

Obviously, the worst choice is the student loan; the best is to start saving early. In that way, neither the student nor the parents will be stuck with a huge debt to repay or loss of current income from investments. Because of the tax advantages of the UGMA, Uncle Sam literally helps pay the student's way through college.

THE GERMANS' LAWS ABOUT CHILDREN ☐

- If you think your kids don't know the value of money, try giving them a nickel.
- The trouble with our children is that they are just as thoughtless, lazy, and silly as we were.
- Children may be deductible, but they are also taxing.

For People Who Work and Manage Their Own Money—Strengthening Your Money Power

WHEN IT COMES TO MONEY, have you ever wished that you could leap tall buildings at a single bound when you know that you have trouble going up the steps? Or have you wished that you could talk to the angels when all you can do is talk to yourself?

When it comes to money, you have two choices: You can develop your financial strength and beat the system, or you can stay weak and let it beat you. Some of the advice included here has been mentioned in other chapters of this book; some has not. What has been mentioned before is so important that it's worth repeating. And all of it is important to anyone in our society who must earn a living and who must spend, save, invest, or even give away money.

MAXIMIZE YOUR EARNINGS

Earn as much as you can consistent with your staying happy. Some people spend their entire lives doing nothing but trying to accumulate more money—and that's fine, if that's what you enjoy. Most people would rather have less money and fewer worries. But it is important to earn as much as you can within the limits of your lifestyle. Surprisingly few people, especially women, will ask the boss for a raise even if it is deserved, and even fewer will switch to more lucrative positions. A case in point: Some years ago, a struggling junior executive in a Philadelphia bank refused an offer to switch to a job that paid double his current income and offered much greater opportunities. Why did he turn down the offer? He felt that the new employer was in a shaky business. The business? A large bank that lacked only the Main Line prestige of his current employer! (It's interesting that new businesses are starting up at a faster rate than ever before in history. Over 25 percent of these businesses are owned by women who became tired of economic discrimination on the job.)

Another aspect of earning money involves putting your savings dollars to work for you. If you accumulate $10,000 in savings, you can keep it in a cookie jar, earning nothing; you can put it into a regular savings account at the bank where it will earn about $550 a year; you can put it into bank certificates of deposit where it will earn perhaps $800 to $1,000 a year or more; or you can invest it in sound common stocks and let your savings earn anywhere from $1,000 to $2,000 a year or more.

Finally, don't forget fringe benefits as an important part of your earnings. Fringe benefits often equal in value as much as one-third of a person's gross income, and best of all, they are "paid" in before-tax dollars. Thus, if you are in the 25 percent marginal tax bracket and your employer provides you with benefits worth $3,000 a year at no out-of-pocket cost to you, it's the same as getting an extra $4,000 a year in gross pay. As long as the government doesn't tax fringe benefits, you're often better off accepting them rather than higher pay, *if* you are making a high enough cash income and *if* the fringe benefits are really useful to you. Especially with two-income families, there is a great danger that benefits provided by the employers of both husband and wife may overlap. For this reason, it is sometimes better if one spouse takes a job with few benefits and gets a higher salary instead.

Whether your concern is with your salary and wages,

your fringe benefits, or with your investment earnings, have the guts to fight or switch jobs to earn the income you deserve. The following sections will give you a summary of tips that can help.

UNDERSTAND MONEY

1. *Be businesslike.* Mary, the accountant, keeps meticulous records for her company and watches its income and costs, but she is very careless about her own money affairs. Why? Because her company earns over $1 million a year and she earns $30,000, so in her mind the company is more important than she is. But she's wrong. Mary doesn't realize it, but she's in business just as much as the company for which she works. It sells its product or service to the public; she sells her skills and time to it. Her income isn't as great as the company's, but relative to her expenses and obligations, it's just as important in her life as her company's income is in its corporate life.

2. *Understand the time value of money.* Everyone thinks that life insurance companies win by tilting the odds of life and death in their favor, and that's true. But they also win in two other ways. First, they get premiums in today's dollars and pay claims in tomorrow's inflated dollars. Second, while they are amassing the dollars to pay future claims, they invest that money and earn income from it. What they do is use the time value of money to make more money—and so should you. Realize, for example, that $1,000 invested today will grow to $2,750 in 10 years, assuming an investment at 10 percent compounded daily.

3. *Understand the concept of opportunity cost.* When you spend money on any good or service, that money is no longer available for investment or for the purchase of any other good or service. Therefore, you

should ask yourself, "Do I want this more than anything else I could get with the money?" The opportunity cost can be calculated by comparing the potential reward from any spending with the best possible rewards obtainable for the same money. For example, if you spend a penny on candy, you get the immediate enjoyment of the candy. But if you invest the penny at 10 percent annual interest, it will grow to 2.6 cents in 10 years, to 4.2 cents in 15 years, to 6.7 cents in 20 years, and to 17.4 cents in 30 years. Spending a penny today means losing the opportunity to invest that penny, allowing it to grow to much more in years to come. And if you spend $2 for a drink, it will yield a fleeting pleasure, whereas if you spend the $2 on a magazine, it might provide entertainment for several hours. This doesn't mean you shouldn't buy candy or drinks, it simply means you should weigh relative benefits from alternate spending choices.

4. *Avoid a "garage sale mentality,"* which means buying the latest fad at top dollar, then selling it for peanuts—or giving it away—when the public interest changes. Drive down any suburban street on a warm, sunny weekend day and you'll see people selling things at garage sales they once couldn't wait to buy. The sad part is that so many of them think they're shrewd to be getting back 10 cents or less on every dollar they once spent.

5. *Avoid living up to your own self-image.* It isn't keeping up with the Joneses that hurts people, it's living up to their own egos. Know where you stand financially and adjust your life-style accordingly.

6. *Allow for unexpected expenses.* Everything always costs more than you think it will.

7. *Finally, don't allow yourself to be ripped off.* A maxim that beats the con artist every time is, "If a deal looks too good to be true, it probably is."

SAVE AND INVEST

There's an old pitch that life insurance salespeople have traditionally used to peddle expensive insurance protection. It starts like this: "Part of everything you earn should be yours to keep . . ." And though life insurance isn't the best way to get to keep it, the premise is true.

You should save part of your income regularly. Accumulate the amount you save in a regular savings account, then as soon as you get enough—say, $500 or more—transfer your savings to a higher-interest account, either a bank certificate of deposit or a money market mutual fund. Accumulate the equivalent of two to six months' income in this type of savings, then start adding investments to your life.

Most people equate investing with the stock market. Here are some tips that will help you do well in the market, although they probably won't make you rich:

1. *Invest for the long haul.* Don't expect miracles, especially overnight.

2. *Invest in quality stocks.* Don't listen to tips. Buy stocks in companies with a solid record of growth, a progressive management, and a good earnings history. Try to choose stocks that consistently pay a good dividend. To really be safe, buy stocks with a ratio of price to earnings of seven-to-one or lower and with a book (or liquidation) value that exceeds the current price.

3. *Buy stocks that reputable analysts expect to grow in value in the next few years.*

4. *Try mutual funds* if buying individual stocks makes you nervous. You can find funds that specialize in any type of investment that suits your interests, ranging from bonds to growth stocks to income stocks. And

you can invest in stocks of companies that don't discriminate against blacks or women, that don't pollute the environment, or that don't build aggressive weaponry.

5. *Avoid real estate investments, commodity futures and options, and stock options* unless you are really affluent and know what you're doing. The potential for gain is great, but so is the potential for loss. All too often, only the experts win.

PRACTICE RISK MANAGEMENT

When financial planners use the term "risk management," they mean life, property, and casualty insurance. But it should mean more than that to you, including the following:

1. *Don't risk living on two incomes if there is any chance that a pregnancy could occur.* Many happy homes have become debtor's prisons through unplanned pregnancies. If there is a possibility of pregnancy, get used to living on the husband's income and banking the wife's.

2. *Plan for child-raising and educational costs.* The "we'll cross that bridge when we come to it" syndrome has kept many couples in penury until late middle age.

3. *Understand any legal documents you sign.* If you don't, you're taking an enormous but avoidable risk. If you need to, ask a knowledgeable friend to explain a document to you.

4. *Cover your life, health, and property with insurance, but don't overdo it.* When it comes to life insurance, buy inexpensive term coverage and invest your savings. Or if you find that difficult, buy variable life and let the insurance company handle the investments at your direction. When it comes to property and casualty insurance, remember that most insurance payouts are for

small amounts, so the companies charge accordingly. The first few hundred dollars of coverage cost much more than the higher coverages. So you can beat the system by taking the maximum deductible allowed while buying higher coverages for total risk. In that way, you'll be covered against the possibility of real financial disaster. And what you save on premiums will soon add up to enough to cover your deductibles.

GET READY FOR RETIREMENT

Have sufficient retirement savings to let you live comfortably without relying too much on Social Security or a company pension. Here's a rule of thumb: You will need about 75 percent of your preretirement income on which to live comfortably; of this amount, you will get about 20 percent from Social Security. This means you must make up the shortfall yourself or be prepared either to live in penury or get help from your children. The following table shows how much you will need to have saved, assuming that your savings can earn 10 percent interest per year:

Savings Needed to Provide 55 percent of Current Income*

Current Income	Retirement Income Needed	Amount of Savings Needed
$20,000	$15,000	$110,000
25,000	18,750	137,500
30,000	22,500	165,000
40,000	30,000	220,000
50,000	37,500	275,000

* Assuming that Social Security will add another 20 percent and that savings will earn 10 percent annual interest

In planning for your retirement years:

1. ***Don't overlook your assets, including the equity you have in your home.*** As mentioned in Chapter 11, equity can be tapped through a reverse annuity mortgage, in states where they are available. RAMs provide a way for a lender to advance a retired homeowner a certain amount of income per month until the property is eventually sold, at which time the loan plus interest (and usually a portion of any gain in equity) must be repaid. And don't forget, if you are over 55 and sell your home, you can take a one-time federal tax exemption of up to $125,000 of the profit from the sale of a personal residence. This can really help to fund your retirement.

2. ***Open an IRA.*** Although every employed person in the country is eligible to have an IRA for both himself or herself and a spouse, only about one person in seven does. IRAs have been mentioned in other chapters. Now, here's a summary of how they help strengthen your money power:

- Deposits made to an IRA are federal income tax-deductible. This means you subtract the total annual contribution from your earned income before calculating your tax liability. Thus, deposits to an IRA reduce your federal tax bite, which has the same effect as increasing your income.
- Earnings as well as deposits for an IRA are tax-deferred, which means that you don't pay any taxes on this money until you actually withdraw it. All bank investments compound at least annually; and carefully chosen stock investments tend to grow at an increasing rate. So there is a multiplier effect that, in the long term, makes sound tax-deferred investments outpace the inflation rate and that actually negates a portion of the eventual tax liability as well. If, at the age of 35, for example, you save $2,000 a year,

assuming that your money earns 10 percent interest per year, you'll have accumulated $349,550 in 30 years; if you're 45 when you begin, you'll amass $121,710 by age 65; if you start when you're 55, the amount will grow to $33,867. Obviously, the earlier a person begins, the better.

In other words, you will someday have to pay taxes on the money you have contributed and on the accrued income, but you'll pay those taxes with dollars whose increased earnings will actually cover a portion of the taxes when they are due. Also, the taxes, being paid at a later date, will be paid in inflated dollars.

· You may roll over all or part of your IRA from one trustee to another once a year without penalty if you reinvest it within 60 days. This means that you can, at any time, borrow your own savings for 60 days without having to pay interest on the "loan." Also, if you keep your IRA savings in bank CDs, it's a good idea to use several small certificates rather than one large-denomination CD. Then, should you need to cash in a portion, you'll have to pay much lower early withdrawal penalties.

· Because increased IRA limits are under serious consideration, check your bank or investment house for the latest deposit limits.

3. Open a tax-deferred employee retirement plan where you work, if you can. This may be through an employer-sponsored participation in a Keogh Plan, a 401K Plan, or a Simplified Employee Pension (SEP) plan. Essentially, with a 401K or an SEP, you get all of the benefits of an IRA plus an employer contribution on which you do not have to pay taxes; *and* you can still have an IRA for additional tax benefits. If you should leave your job, you do not lose the amount deposited, nor are there any time-on-the-job requirements. If you work for a nonprofit organization, you can open an employee retirement plan through a tax-deferred annuity and have an IRA in addition.

4. *Open a Keogh Plan account if you're self-employed.* The benefits are practically the same as for an IRA, except that you can't make yourself a rollover loan. Also, if you make an early withdrawal from a Keogh Plan, you are further penalized by not being allowed to make any more deposits for five years. However, as outlined in Chapter 11, you have the option of making much higher deposit limits in a Keogh than in an IRA; in fact, depending on your self-employment income, the annual deposit limits for a Keogh Plan can be 15 times as high. Here, too, you may have an IRA in addition to a Keogh Plan.

REDUCE ESTATE AND INHERITANCE TAXES

Estate planning has many facets, but the one that causes the most concern is reduction of tax burden. The theory goes like this: John and Mary worked hard all of their lives and paid taxes on every cent of income they earned. As they prospered and made investments, they paid taxes on the earnings that were generated. When they died, both the federal and state governments again taxed the same dollars on which they had already paid full income taxes. Unfair? Perhaps, but there are ways to eliminate or at least to reduce some of those taxes.

First, realize the difference between the types of death taxes. Estate taxes are imposed by the federal government and are paid by the estate before any distribution of assets is made. Inheritance taxes are imposed by the state government against specific heirs and are paid from the share of the estate they are to receive. This means that the savings strategies for federal and state taxes differ somewhat. If your estate exceeds $100,000 —and if you own your own home it almost certainly does—get the advice of a tax accountant or attorney. In any case, these tips should help:

1. *Above all, have a proper will drawn by an attorney.* Holographic wills (those in the handwriting of the person making the will) are admissible in some states and inadmissible in others. Either way, they can be more easily contested and expensive to probate than regular wills.

2. *Don't rely on joint ownership to save probate costs.* Joint ownership usually doesn't succeed in doing this, and it can even delay the administration of an estate and increase the costs.

3. *Establish your domicile in only one state.* This is vitally important! Many people have a home in one state and a winter or summer home in another. They get careless about where they register to vote and get their driver's licenses. Thus, when they die, both states may claim them as residents and inheritance taxes may have to be paid in both. To avoid this, you should register to vote and get your driver's license in the state that you wish to be considered your legal residence. Leave a notarized letter stating your intent to be a resident of that state. Make certain the attorney who draws up your will does so in the state of your domicile and knows of your intent.

The federal estate tax law gives a total marital exemption from taxes on assets left to a surviving spouse. So federal taxes usually impact most in the case of children who are left an inheritance by the last parent to die. State inheritance taxes vary widely, but generally give a large exclusion to surviving spouses, a lesser one to surviving children, still less to other relatives, and the smallest to nonrelatives.

In any event, to reduce the impact of taxes on your estate, you may give away assets during your lifetime, with an annual exclusion from gift taxes, of up to $10,000 per person, or $20,000 per person if you are married and file income taxes jointly. This is an excellent way to give money or property to your children or grandchildren. You also may set up a trust that may be testamentary (it takes effect at your death), or an *inter vivos,* or living, trust, which may be revocable (you may change it during your lifetime) or irrevocable (you may not change it). A revocable trust avoids only the expenses and delays of probate; an irrevocable trust removes assets from your estate and thus from taxation—but you lose control of those assets while you're still living.

The secret of estate planning, as with all financial planning, is simply to look ahead. Thinking about your own demise isn't pleasant, but it should be done at least once to assure that what you have worked so hard to earn and save can be passed on to those you love.

THE GERMANS' LAWS FOR PEOPLE WHO WORK AND MANAGE THEIR OWN MONEY

- If an item is advertised for "less than $50," the price will always be $49.95.
- When people are young, they look for the pot of gold at the end of the rainbow; when they're older, often all they have is the pot.
- You can't take it with you, but while you're here there aren't many places you can go without it.

Glossary

adjusted gross income The figure on a person's federal income tax form that is calculated by subtracting adjustments to income from total income. Adjustments include such items as Individual Retirement Account contributions, penalties on early withdrawals of savings, alimony payments, and the deduction for a married couple when both work. Some of these adjustments may be changed under proposed new tax laws.

alimony Money to help cover living expenses paid following a divorce to a former spouse by his or her ex-wife or ex-husband, the payment of which may be in a lump sum, through a trust, or in monthly installments. Alimony payments are tax deductible by the person who pays them and are taxable for those who receive them. A person who does not receive wages may count alimony as earned income for purposes of contributing to an Individual Retirement Account.

alimony trust A trust fund, set up through a trustee, usually a bank, from which alimony payments are made.

annual percentage rate (APR) The yearly rate of interest charged for a loan, which all lenders, under the truth-in-lending provisions of the Consumer Credit Protection Act of 1968, must calculate in a uniform manner and so advertise in order that consumers can compare rates. Determining the APR for a specified amount to be borrowed for a specified period of time is complicated, so the Federal Reserve makes standard rate charts available for lenders to use. These charts also help lenders to avoid penalty-causing mistakes.

annuity An investment for which the investor later receives regular payments for life or for a specified period of time.

The amount paid out is based on the earnings of the money invested and the life expectancy of the investor. *Tax-deferred annuities* have similar advantages to those of Individual Retirement Accounts in that premiums are tax-deductible and the earnings grow tax-free until payments are made. If a person works for a qualified nonprofit organization, he or she may have a tax-deferred annuity in addition to an IRA.

asset Anything a person owns that has value, such as cash, investments, real estate, and money or property owed to that person by someone else.

automatic overdraft account A checking or NOW account that enables the customer to overdraw the account by writing checks for more money than is on deposit, thus creating a loan up to a specified limit. The amount of the loan made in this way, plus interest, must be repaid by the borrower and is commonly charged to the customer's credit-card account with the bank. See the section in Chapter 9 titled "How to Get a Quick Loan" for more information about the use of this type of account.

bankruptcy (personal) A declaration by a court of law that a person is financially insolvent. The Bankruptcy Reform Act of 1978 offers such a person the chance to file for debt reorganization under Chapter 13 of the law or to accept outright voluntary personal bankruptcy under Chapter 7. For information about these two provisions, see the section of Chapter 3 titled "How to Spell Relief."

beneficiary The recipient of the proceeds under a will, trust, or life insurance policy.

bill-payer loan A loan made for the purpose of repaying other loans; also called a *consolidation loan*. Such a borrower uses the money to pay off his or her smaller loans, then has one payment to make each month instead of many. Ideally, the money is borrowed for a time long enough to make each payment smaller than the total amount formerly paid out each month.

bond, corporate An interest-paying certificate of indebtedness issued by a corporation. Because the value of such bonds can vary widely, an investor should know what he or she is doing before buying them.

bond, tax-free An interest-paying certificate of indebtedness issued by a state or local government, the earnings for which are exempt from federal taxation and sometimes from state taxation.

bond, U.S. savings An interest-paying non-negotiable certificate of indebtedness issued by the U.S. government. Savings bonds are sold in denominations of from $50 to $10,000. The purchase price for *EE bonds* is 50 percent of their face value, which is paid when they mature; the time needed to reach maturity varies as the interest rate changes. *HH bonds* are sold for their full face value and mature in 10 years; interest is paid every six months.

book value The value of a share of common stock in the event that the company involved goes out of business. This is calculated by dividing the value of the assets of the company by the number of shares outstanding. The book value is usually lower than the market value. Some investors use this figure as an investment guide, believing that a stock is a relatively safe buy if the market value is at or below the book value.

capital appreciation The growth in the value of an investment asset, such as a home, common stock, or certificate of deposit.

capital gains The profit made from the sale of an investment asset. *Short-term capital gains* are the profit from the sale of an investment owned for six months or less; *long-term capital gains* are the profit from the sale of an investment owned for a longer period of time. Short-term gains are taxed by the federal government as ordinary income; but 60 percent of long-term gains are exempt from federal taxation, and the maximum tax rate is 50 percent on the remainder.

cash surrender value The amount that an owner of a level-premium permanent life insurance policy would get when cashing in the policy during the lifetime of the person who is insured.

cash value The amount that an owner of level-premium permanent life insurance could borrow against the policy. It is common for old policies to have loan rates as low as 5 or 6 percent.

certificate of deposit (CD) A savings account with a bank, with a specified date of maturity and rate of interest, for which the customer is given a receipt (the certificate) for the amount deposited. Interest rates for CDs are higher than those paid for regular savings accounts. Since there are no legal restrictions on the amounts required for deposit in a CD or the interest rates that banks may pay, it's smart to shop around for the best deal. Generally, the longer the term, the higher the rate of interest that will be paid. If the customer withdraws the money before the CD matures, a penalty is charged.

child support Money paid according to an agreement or a court order for the living expenses of a child by a parent after that person's divorce or separation from the other parent, who retains custody of the child. It is to the advantage of the payer to pay less child support in proportion to any alimony that is paid because child support is not tax-deductible. Nor is it taxable for the receiver. Under the Tax Reform Act of 1984, the parent who has custody of the child can claim the dependency tax deduction regardless of who contributes how much to his or her support. However, this deduction can be waived in writing. And the child's medical expenses are deductible for the parent who pays them, provided they exceed 5 percent of that person's adjusted gross income.

Clifford Trust An agreement under which income-producing property is temporarily transferred to a beneficiary for a period of at least 10 years and a day. Until the trust terminates, the original owner may not use or sell the property; but at the end of the agreed-upon time, ownership reverts to that person. Thus, a Clifford Trust is also known as a *reversionary trust*. For more details, see the section of Chapter 15 titled "Elderly Parents" and the section of Chapter 16 titled "College Costs." Proposed tax changes may reduce benefits.

collateral Security that is pledged to guarantee payment of a loan. An example is a car, which is collateral for the auto loan used to buy it. If a borrower defaults in making the auto loan payments, the lender may repossess the car and sell it to get the balance due on the loan.

commodity futures Contracts to buy or sell a specified amount of a product of trade, such as sugar, soybeans, or precious metals, for a specified price at a specified future date. People who buy the contracts hope that, when the date arrives, the value of the product will have increased enough for them to make a profit. In the meantime, the producers have cash to use immediately.

commodity options The right to buy or sell a commodity futures contract for a specified price during a specified period of time. Speculating in this way usually involves a large amount of money and is very risky.

compound interest Interest that is paid on the principal as well as the accrued interest. Savings account interest may be calculated on a daily, continuous (the results are essentially the same as daily), weekly, monthly, quarterly, semiannual, or annual basis. The more frequently the interest is calculated, the higher the yield will be.

cosign To jointly sign a promissory note so that another person can get a loan. If the borrower fails to repay the loan, the cosigner is responsible for doing so.

creative financing Getting more than one loan to buy a home. A typical deal is that in which the buyer gets a first mortgage from a bank and a second mortgage from the seller.

credit limit The prearranged maximum amount a person or firm is entitled to borrow. Thus, if an individual has a $2,000 limit on his or her bank credit card, he or she may not accrue an outstanding bill for more than $2,000. Monthly credit-card statements usually give the customer the amount he or she may still spend before reaching the credit limit.

credit rating The standing of a person or firm in terms of borrowing capabilities, based on past performance in the repayment of loans; or the amount a lender believes a borrower has the ability to repay.

custodial account An account set up under the rules of the Uniform Gifts to Minors Act at a bank or brokerage house. Also see the definition for *Uniform Gifts to Minors Act (UGMA)* in this glossary and the section of Chapter 16 titled

"College Costs." The benefits of UGMA accounts may be limited under proposed tax law changes.

debt The money, goods, or services that are owed to someone else.

debt counselor A professional advisor for people who are in debt. See the section of Chapter 3 titled "How to Spell Relief" for details on how to contact a member agency of the National Foundation for Consumer Credit. So that a responsible agency will be available to help debtors pay their bills, banks and other lenders contribute money to this organization. Therefore, people who use its services have to pay very little.

disclosure statement A statement that all lenders, under the truth-in-lending provisions of the Consumer Credit Protection Act of 1968, must give a borrower when a loan is made, setting forth the terms of the loan, including the annual percentage rate and the finance charge.

dividends A portion of net profits that companies pay to their stockholders; the interest paid on savings accounts by savings and loan associations that are mutually owned by depositors; earnings from money market mutual funds; a refund of excess premiums from a whole life insurance policy.

domicile A person's legal residence. See the section of Chapter 17 titled "Reduce Estate and Inheritance Taxes" for an explanation of why, if someone owns homes in two states, it is important to establish his or her domicile in only one of them.

dun To make repeated demands for the payment of a bill. See the section of Chapter 3 titled "How to Spell Relief" for details of what a bill collector is not allowed to do under the provisions of the Fair Credit Reporting Act.

equity The difference between the value of an asset, such as a home, and the amount of the outstanding balance due on any loans. For example, if a home is valued at $85,000 and the buyer still owes $25,000 on the mortgage, the equity amounts to $60,000.

exemptions, personal The portion of taxable income that is exempt from federal taxation. One exemption can be claimed for each person who files a return, for his or her spouse if filing a joint return, and for each qualified dependent. Extra exemptions are allowed for specified age and blindness conditions, although the Reagan Administration has proposed eliminating these.

finance charge The total amount in dollars charged for a loan, which all lenders, under the truth-in-lending provision of the Consumer Credit Protection Act of 1968, must disclose to a borrower when making the loan. The longer it takes to repay a loan, the higher the finance charge will be.

financial planner A professional advisor in the management or transaction of money matters. Financial planners range from highly to poorly trained individuals, who charge flat fees or who earn commissions on the insurance policies or stock they sell to their clients.

401K Plan A retirement plan to which both the employee and his or her employer deposit up to a maximum combined annual contribution of 25 percent of the employee's salary or $30,000, whichever is less. Limits may be reduced under proposed tax law changes.

fringe benefit An advantage of employment, such as free health insurance, that an employee receives in addition to his or her pay. See the section of Chapter 17 titled "Maximize Your Earnings" for a discussion of fringe benefits versus higher pay. Some fringe benefits may be taxed under proposed tax law changes.

health maintenance organization (HMO)—An organization, usually sponsored by a hospital or a medical clinic, that provides health insurance coverage for members who pay a fee to belong.

Individual Retirement Account (IRA) An account in which retirement funds up to a specified annual maximum may be voluntarily deposited by an employed person and his or her spouse into a government-approved plan at a bank, savings institution, or brokerage house. Under the provisions of the

Economic Recovery Tax Act of 1981, the amount deposited may be deducted from taxable income, and taxes on the income earned through the investment are deferred. Taxes are paid later as sums are withdrawn for retirement, by which time the person is likely to be in a lower bracket. In the meantime, the tax-free compounding of interest means that the money grows at an accelerated rate. Money in an IRA may be withdrawn without penalty at age 59½, and withdrawals must begin by age 70½. For more details, see the Section of Chapter 17 titled "Get Ready for Retirement."

inflation An economic condition characterized by a general rise in price levels resulting in a decrease in purchasing power. During inflation, people who must live on a fixed income and those whose increases in income don't keep pace with the increases in prices suffer the most.

insurance, auto A plan for sharing the costs of personal injury and property damage caused by or to automobiles under which the owners of automobiles contribute to a common fund from which claims are paid. *Collision insurance* is that section of an auto insurance policy that covers losses to the insured person's car in the event that he or she has an accident and is unable to collect from the other driver or his or her insurance company. *Comprehensive coverage* is for losses to the insured person's car if it is stolen or damaged by such things as fire, hail, or vandalism. The higher the deductibles, or the amounts the insured must pay if he or she has a loss before the insurance company will pay a claim, the lower his or her insurance premiums will be.

insurance, casualty Liability insurance, of which auto insurance is the most common type.

insurance, endowment Life insurance for which premiums are paid for a specified period of time, commonly 10 or 20 years, after which the amount of the face value of the policy is paid to the insured person. If that person should die before the end of the time period, his or her beneficiary gets the amount of the face value.

insurance, health A plan for sharing the costs of medical expenses under which those who are insured contribute to a common fund from which claims are paid. Such plans are offered by Blue Cross/Blue Shield, Medicare, commercial insurers, and health maintenance organizations (HMOs).

insurance, homeowner's A plan for sharing the costs of damage to houses and other residential structures and injuries to people under which those who are insured contribute to a common fund from which claims are paid. Some of the losses that are not covered are those deliberately caused by the insured, those that are a result of business pursuits of the insured, vandalism when the property has been left vacant for over 30 days, and environmental pollution.

insurance, level-premium permanent A life insurance policy in which premiums are for the same amount during the life of the policy, which continues in force as long as the premiums are paid and the insured person lives. Level-premium insurance is also referred to as *whole, straight life, ordinary,* or *cash-value* insurance.

insurance, life A plan for pooling money from a number of people so that benefits can be paid to the beneficiary of each policyholder when that policyholder dies. Thus, the beneficiary is protected from loss caused by the death of the insured. Many life insurance policies also include savings features.

insurance premium The payment, made on a periodic basis, that is due on an insurance policy.

insurance, property A plan for sharing the costs of losses to the policyholder's property, or those suffered by other people or their property when the policyholder is responsible, under which those who are insured contribute to a common fund from which claims are paid. The most common types are homeowner's and tenant's insurance.

insurance, straight life Level-premium permanent life insurance, which is also referred to as *whole, ordinary,* or *cash-value* life insurance.

insurance, tenant's Homeowner's insurance that covers the loss or theft of a renter's belongings. Liability protection and riders to cover jewelry and other valuables may also be included.

insurance, term Life insurance that provides protection for a specified period of time, such as three or five years, under which no savings feature is included. When a person is younger, premiums for term insurance are less expensive than they are when he or she gets older. Both premiums and agents' commissions are lower for this type of life insurance than they are for level-premium insurance.

insurance, whole life Level-premium permanent life insurance, which is also referred to as *straight life, ordinary,* or *cash-value* insurance.

joint ownership Ownership of property by more than one person. See the section of Chapter 13 titled "Joint Ownership—Some Definitions" for an explanation of right of survivorship, tenancy by the entirety, tenancy in common, and joint tenancy.

Keogh Plan A plan under which retirement funds up to a specified annual maximum may be voluntarily deposited by a self-employed person into a government-approved account. As with an Individual Retirement Account, the amount deposited may be deducted from taxable income, and taxes on the income earned through the investment are deferred, allowing earnings to grow at an accelerated rate. If a self-employed person has full-time employees who have worked for him or her for three or more years, the employer must also contribute the same percentage of their incomes as he or she does of his or her own income into a Keogh Plan for each of them. For more details about this plan, see the section of Chapter 11 titled "Preparing for Old Age."

lease A contract between a person who rents property and the owner of the property that sets forth the terms of the rental, such as the length of time the property may be used, the amount to be paid, who is responsible for repairs, and many other specifications.

liability Any money that is owed, which includes payments for bills, taxes, loans, or any other financial obligation.

load A fee, usually charged at the time of purchase, to cover the cost of the sales commission when buying mutual fund shares. The rate charged is usually between 6 and 8 percent of the amount spent on the securities. A *low-load* fee is normally between 3 and 4 percent. A *no-load* mutual fund is one for which no sales commission is charged.

marginal tax bracket The federal income tax rate that is charged on the last $100 you earn. This is important because deductions are subtracted from these last dollars. If, for example, a person is in the 35 percent marginal tax bracket, he or she can save $35 for every $100 in additional deductions he or she can take. A person's tax bracket, therefore, is not, as some think, the percentage of income that he or she pays in taxes.

market index option A form of stock market speculation by which a person has the right to buy or sell an index contract or a futures contract for a certain price at a certain time. An index is arrived at by a particular organization by determining the average price of a particular group of stocks. The Standard & Poor's 500 Index, for example, is arrived at by adding up the prices of all the shares of its 500 stocks and dividing by 500; it is an index on which options are commonly traded.

market value The price that can be received when selling a home or other piece of property.

marriage penalty The slightly higher federal income taxes that must be paid by married couples compared to single persons. Under the Economic Recovery Tax Act of 1981, however, in cases in which married couples both work and file a joint return, 10 percent may be deducted from the earned income of the spouse with the lower earnings, up to a maximum of $3,000. This helps to offset the marriage penalty. This deduction may be eliminated, however, under proposed tax law changes.

Medicaid Federal and state assistance for the needy to pay medical expenses. Recipients are generally people who receive public assistance or Supplemental Security Income (SSI).

Medicare Government-sponsored health insurance for people aged 65 or over to help pay medical expenses.

Mini-Keogh A Keogh Plan under which a person with self-employment income who makes $15,000 or less a year from all sources may save up to $750 a year or 100 percent of his or her self-employment income, whichever is less, in a government-approved account.

money market mutual fund A mutual fund that puts deposits into money market investments, such as bank certificates of deposit, Treasury bills, loans to corporations, and Eurodollars. Deposits in these funds are not insured, but the investments are of high enough quality to make them safe.

mortgage The legal document that pledges property as security for the loan made to purchase it.

mutual fund An open-end investment trust under which people pool their money for investment in a variety of securities. Investors may put more money into the fund or take it out at the current market rate at any time. Mutual funds give people with small amounts of money to invest the chance to put it into a diversity of stocks, bonds, or other vehicles at reduced brokerage fees.

net worth The total value of the amount owned minus the total value of the amount owed, i.e., all of a person's assets minus all of his or her liabilities. To calculate your personal net worth, use the chart provided in Chapter 1 titled "Financial Fitness Profile."

NOW account An interest-paying account that looks and works like a checking account but is legally a kind of savings account from which withdrawals can be made using a draft called a *negotiable order of withdrawal*. The purpose of this type of account is to avoid the regulation under the Banking Act of 1933 that prohibits the payment of interest on checking accounts. NOW accounts rates, set by law at a maximum of 5.25 percent interest, are no longer to be regulated beginning April 1, 1986.

opportunity cost The extra "cost" of a good or service that the amount spent could have earned if it had been more profitably invested. For example, if $100 were invested at 10 percent interest compounded daily, it would grow to $275.59 over a period of 10 years. Therefore, if a person spent the

$100 on an item he or she really didn't need instead of investing it, in this case the opportunity cost of that item, over a 10-year period, would be $175.59. See the section of Chapter 17 titled "Understand Money" for a more detailed explanation.

passbook savings (or *regular savings*)   An account in which transactions are recorded for the customer in a passbook. Because of the low interest, it is a good idea to use a passbook account for accumulating funds until enough is saved to transfer into a higher yielding investment, such as a bank certificate of deposit or a money market mutual fund.

principal   The face value of an investment or of a check, note, or bond; an amount that has been invested, not counting any earnings or profit.

probate   The certification of the authenticity of a will by a court of law and, when needed, the action taken to make sure that the terms of a will are carried out or that an estate is settled when a person dies without a will.

promissory note   A written promise to repay a debt. Such a statement should include the amount of money involved, the date when it is payable, where and to whom the money is to be paid, and the signature of the borrower.

real estate   Property in land and buildings. Real estate includes things attached to the land, such as trees, shrubs, and fences, and built-in necessities in buildings, such as a furnace, a stove, and bathroom fixtures.

reverse annuity mortgage (RAM)   A plan, available in some states, that allows a homeowner who lives in an area where property values are increasing to supplement retirement income by tapping the equity in his or her home. The lender advances to the homeowner a certain amount of money each month until he or she dies or the property is sold, after which the loan plus interest plus, typically, a portion of the increase in the value of the home, are repaid to the lender. This means, of course, that the amount left to the homeowner's heirs will be reduced, but it could make the difference between a comfortable retirement and living in poverty. See the section of Chapter 11 titled "Preparing for Old Age" for information about RAMs as well as the receipt of one-time tax-free capital gains on the sale of a house.

right of recision The right, under the truth-in-lending provision of the Consumer Credit Protection Act of 1968 as well as some state laws, to cancel an installment purchase contract within three business days and to get back any money a person has paid. The right of recision applies to anything the person agrees to buy on credit for which his or her home is used as collateral or, under the Federal Trade Commission, to anything a person buys from a door-to-door salesperson, such as home improvements.

rollover The renewal of a loan agreement to extend the length of time required for its maturity; the transfer of assets from one investment to another. For example, under the Economic Recovery Tax Act of 1981, taxes can be deferred on the profits from the sale of a principal residence if those profits are rolled over into buying another residence within a two-year period.

Simplified Employee Pension (SEP) plan A retirement plan to which both the employee and his or her employer contribute. Under an SEP, no taxes are required to be paid on the portion contributed by the employer, which may be up to $30,000 a year or 15 percent of the employee's salary, whichever is less. And the portion contributed by the employee—which may be up to $2,000 or 100 percent of his or her salary, whichever is less—may be treated the same for tax purposes as amounts put into an IRA. For more information, see the section of Chapter 17 titled "Get Ready for Retirement."

speculate To take risks in buying and selling securities, commodities, options, and other investments in order to make large gains.

stock, common Shares in the ownership of a corporation for which one share represents the right to receive one part of the corporation's distributed earnings and the right to vote at shareholders' meetings.

stock, growth Common stock that is expected to grow in value, but that is not expected to pay relatively high current dividends. This type of stock is more speculative than income stock.

stock, income Common stock that pays regular, relatively high current dividends.

stock option A contract for the right to buy *(call option)* or sell *(put option)* shares of a particular stock at a specified price on or before a specified date. Each option, which represents 100 shares of stock, can be bought for a fraction of the cost of the original shares, giving the investor much greater potential for profit or loss. However, they are risky in that the entire amount invested can be lost.

stock, preferred Shares in the ownership of a corporation for which the shareholder gets certain preferential treatment, such as precedence in receiving dividends. Shareholders, however, have no voting rights unless dividends are in default. Preferred stocks often offer high income, but common stocks have the potential for offering higher capital gains as well.

stock, utility Shares of stock in a company that provides public service, such as gas or electricity.

substantial penalty for early withdrawal The penalties set by law that are assessed for withdrawing the funds in a certificate of deposit before its date of maturity. For CDs of one year or less, the penalty is loss of one month's interest; for CDs of over a year, the penalty is loss of three months' interest. These amounts are tax-deductible on federal Form 1040.

taxable income A person's adjusted gross income minus deductions and exemptions.

tax deduction An expense that legally may be deducted from income when computing federal income taxes. Each deduction reduces taxable income.

tax-deferred payment A tax payment that is put off until a later date. With an Individual Retirement Account, Keogh Plan, Simplified Employee Pension plan, 401K Plan, or a tax-deferred annuity, the money invested grows tax-free until after retirement.

tax, estate Federal tax on the assets of a deceased person, which must be paid before the assets are distributed to his or her heirs.

tax, excise A tax on the manufacture, sale, or consumption of certain products; or a tax on the privilege to do something, such as take part in a particular business.

tax, inheritance State tax on the assets of a deceased person, which is paid from the shares of the estate that his or her heirs are to receive.

tax, property A tax made by a local government based on a percentage of the assessed valuation of the property.

tax, regressive A tax that impacts the most on those who can least afford to pay it. A sales tax is an example of a regressive tax.

tax shelter A way to legally avoid paying a part of one's federal income tax by taking advantage of certain laws. The biggest tax shelter for middle-income people is a primary residence, because the mortgage interest payments are tax-deductible and a large portion of increased value is tax-exempt.

Treasury securities U.S. government obligations that are sold to the public through the Federal Reserve Banks, either at a bank for a fee or directly from a Federal Reserve Bank for no fee. These safe investments include Treasury bills (T-bills), Treasury bonds, Treasury certificates, and Treasury notes.

trust, *inter vivos* A *living trust*; a trust that is set up through the assets of a living person, under which assets are entrusted for the benefit of someone else.

trust, irrevocable A trust that can't be changed or cancelled by the person who establishes it.

trust, reversionary A trust under which the assets revert to the original owner at the end of a specified period of time. Also see the definition for Clifford Trust, the section of Chapter 15 titled "Elderly Parents," and the section of Chapter 16 titled "College Costs."

trust, testamentary A trust set up under the terms of a will that takes effect at the death of the person who establishes it. A trustee, often a bank, is appointed to manage the assets of the deceased person for his or her beneficiary.

truth-in-lending (TIL)   The informal title for the Consumer
Credit Protection Act of 1968.

unemployment compensation   An insurance plan, the premiums for which are paid through employer assessments,
that provides income for people who suffer job layoffs.

Uniform Gifts to Minors Act (UGMA)   A law that allows income from an irrevocable trust set up for a minor to be taxed
to the minor rather than the person who established the trust.
When the minor becomes an adult, the assets go to him or
her to use as he or she wishes. The tax-free growth of income
in a UGMA account makes it an excellent way to save money
for a child's college education. See the section of Chapter 16
titled "College Costs" for more information. The benefits of
UGMA accounts may be limited under proposed tax law
changes.

will   A legal document that sets forth the details of the way a
person's estate is to be distributed after his or her death. To
avoid legal complications, it is best to have an attorney draw
up a will.

zero bracket amount   The basic amount of money, which is
built into tax-computation formulas, that the federal government allows a taxpayer as an automatic deduction. For more
information, see the section of Chapter 7 titled "Think Deductions."

Index